Mapping Western Civilization
A Guide for Beginning Students

GERALD A. DANZER
University of Illinois at Chicago

HarperCollins*Publishers*

Executive Editor: Bruce Borland
Developmental Editor: Rebecca W. Strehlow
Project Coordination: Lucy Lesiak Design, Inc.
Cover Design: Lucy Lesiak Design, Inc.
Text Design: Lucy Lesiak Design, Inc.
Photo Research: Judy Ladendorf
Cartographer: Paul Yatabe. Maps produced by
    Mapping Specialists, Inc.
Production: Michael Weinstein
Compositor: Lucy Lesiak Design, Inc.
Printer and Binder: Malloy Lithographing, Inc.
Cover Printer: Malloy Lithographing, Inc.

ACKNOWLEDGMENTS

Cover: National Maritime Museum, Greenwich

Topic 7 From *The History of Cartography*, Vol. I, edited by J. B. Harley and David Woodward. The University of Chicago Press. © 1987 by The University of Chicago. All rights reserved. Published 1987. Printed in the United States of America.

Topic 8 From *Imago Mundi*, Vol. 2, 1937. Reprinted in 1964. © Imago Mundi Limited, Kent, England.

Topic 9 Courtesy Detroit Edison Company

Topic 10 Reprinted from O. A. W. Dilke: *Greek and Roman Maps*. Copyright © 1985 by Thames & Hudson, Ltd., London. Used by permission of the publisher, Cornell University Press.

Topic 11 National Maritime Museum, Greenwich

Topic 14 Courtesy of The Newberry Library, Chicago

Topic 15 The Bodleian Library, Oxford, MS Pococke 375, fols. 3v–4r

Topic 16 By permission of the British Library

Topic 17 Photo: Woodmansterne

Topic 19 From A. E. Nordenskiöld, Facsimile–Atlas to the Early History of Cartography, Stockholm, 1889. Translated from the Swedish orginally by J. A. Ekelöf and C. R. Markham. Copyright © 1973 by Dover Publications Inc.

Topic 21 G. R. Crone, *Maps and Their Makers*. Hamden, CT: Archon Books (Shoestring Press), 1978, p. 77. © G. R. Crone.

Topic 30 From *A Strategic Atlas* by Gerard Chaliand and Jean-Pierre Regeau. Copyright English translation © 1985 by Gerard Chaliand and Jean-Pierre Regeau. Reprinted by permission of HarperCollins Publishers Inc.

Mapping Western Civilization:
A Guide for Beginning Students

ISBN 0-673-53774-9

98 9 8 7 6 5 4

CONTENTS

INTRODUCTION

The three essential ingredients of history are people, place, and time. To be good students of the past, and to effectively operate in the present, we must be familiar with each of these basic dimensions.

People come first, as individuals to be sure, but more importantly in history's eyes, as members of groups and societies. Clio, the muse of history, centers her attention on the experiences of particular groups of people, and she usually employs a story format to tell something about a particular human adventure. Her narratives make suggestions about the meaning and purpose of life by precept, by example, by their structure, and by the way the story is told. Some forms of historical presentation, including textbooks, are often very explicit in their analysis, listing causes and results, explaining the importance of events, or clearly suggesting the meaning of the past for the present. These interpretative features distinguish a historical account from a chronicle, the listing of events in chronological order without the connecting tissue of a narrative or the explicit commentary of a textbook or monograph.

At the college level a history course opens up new worlds for students as they perceive, often for the first time, the depth and richness of the subject. In the course of your study, you will begin to feel the powerful pull of Clio's charms, discovering history as a way of looking at life and the human condition while exploring its fascinating range of interpretative possibilities. History may present difficulties as well. Foremost among these is a sense of frustration.

Beginning students are often overwhelmed by the immensity of the past. How can one keep everything straight? Here is where the other two basic ingredients of history prove their value.

Time and space provide a matrix for locating people and their events so that everything can be kept in order. Dates and places serve as reference points for the immense amount of information found in your textbook.

Mapping Western Civilization is designed to help you put things in order so that your study of the past can move quickly to the fascinating level that wrestles with meaning and significance. This book is partly a handbook, partly a laboratory manual, and partly a study guide. It focuses on places and the spatial context of America's story. Maps are the usual mode of presentation, although timelines appear at regular intervals as a kind of map for temporal affairs.

Mapping Western Civilization expects you to do the job. It asks you to complete the maps and to work out the temporal sequences. It is hoped that you will make discoveries along the way, and that the discipline of systematically going through each topic will help you put things together into a meaningful synthesis. Then, as you break into the clear with a thrill of new insight, don't be afraid to crack a smile of satisfaction or to exclaim: "I see—that's how this stuff fits together!"

Several features occur regularly in this manual. "Places" deals with basic geographical data you will record on an outline map. "Working with Space" leads onward to an understanding of the basic spatial factors present in the activity. "Working with Time" provides a chronological context for your study, using both the diachronic and the synchronic functions of temporal order. The "Extensions" provide an opportunity for you to do a variety of writing projects. In some ways they are the culmination of each lesson.

Where short answers are called for, an answer key is provided in the appendix. However, recording answers is not really at the heart of the process. The lessons focus on developing skills of observation, on analyzing documents, and on bringing various facts or events together in a device that suggests connections between them.

Our goal is to eventually tie the major blocks of time and space together so that you will have a sense of Western civilization as a whole. Then you will be in a position to control the textbook and to use this mastery as a springboard to the real purpose of studying the past: understanding who we are, knowing where we came from, and deciding where we want to go from here. As on any journey, it is best to have a map in your head as well as a map in your hand. *Mapping Western Civilization* is now something for your hand, but its goal is to give you the mental map as well. Bon voyage!

Gerald A. Danzer

Mapping Western Civilization
A Guide for Beginning Students

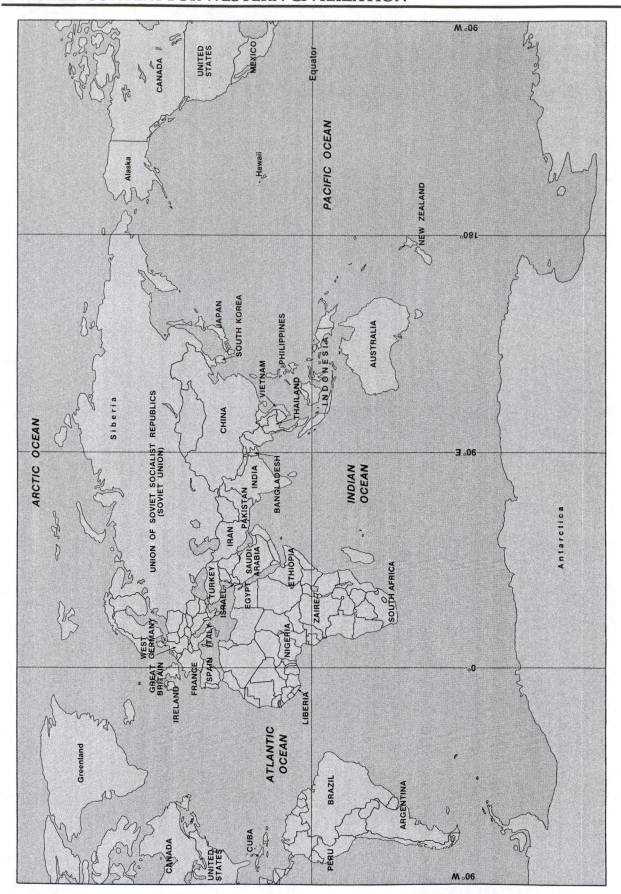

HarperCollins Publishers © 1991

TOPIC 1
A World Context for Western Civilization

BACKGROUND

The migration of peoples, the exchange of goods, the diffusion of ideas, and the quest for new lands are major themes in the story of Western civilization. All of them in the final analysis demand a world map to fully tell the tale. This version is a modification of the classic Mercator projection, which sets the earth's surface in a rectangular grid. Maps using this type of projection have provided the dominant picture of the earth for Western peoples during the past several centuries.

PLACES

1. *Oceans.* According to tradition, the four oceans are labeled on the map. Be sure you can locate them, but notice that there is really only one "World Ocean." Label it on the map in such a way that the name "World Ocean" extends from the Atlantic across the Indian Ocean to the Pacific.

2. *Continents.* Of the continents, only Antarctica is named. Label North America, South America, Africa, Europe, Asia, and Australia.

3. *Meridians.* Four major meridians are given on the map. A meridian is an imaginary line that connects the earth's poles and is perpendicular to the equator. The prime meridian passes through Great Britain, _____ , and _____ as well as several nations in Africa. The 90° east meridian crosses Asia from the Soviet Union on the north to _____ on the south. The _____ meridian marks the approximate location of the International Date Line. The _____ meridian divides the United States along the Mississippi Valley.

4. *Parallels.* The only parallel given on the map is the equator. It touches the mainland of only two continents: _____ and

_____ .

WORKING WITH SPACE

1. South America on the map looks like it is only as large as Greenland. In reality it is over eight times as large. Africa is actually about _____ times the size of Greenland.

2. Another copy of this map is located in the appendix so that you can cut it up and tape it together again with the prime meridian in the center. The usual world map for the study of Western civilization places the prime meridian, a European device, at the center of the map. The result is a Eurocentric map, valuable for many uses, but hardly the only way to put Western civilization in a world context. Note that this map should be cut along the 180° meridian and rearranged to put Europe in the center.

EXTENSIONS

Cutting the projection presents the map as a flexible tool to help us conceive the world from different perspectives. Write a brief essay comparing the image of the world projected by these two maps. Which do you think is the best one for use in a study of Western civilization: the one centered on the prime meridian or the one centered on the Indian Ocean?

HarperCollins Publishers © 1991

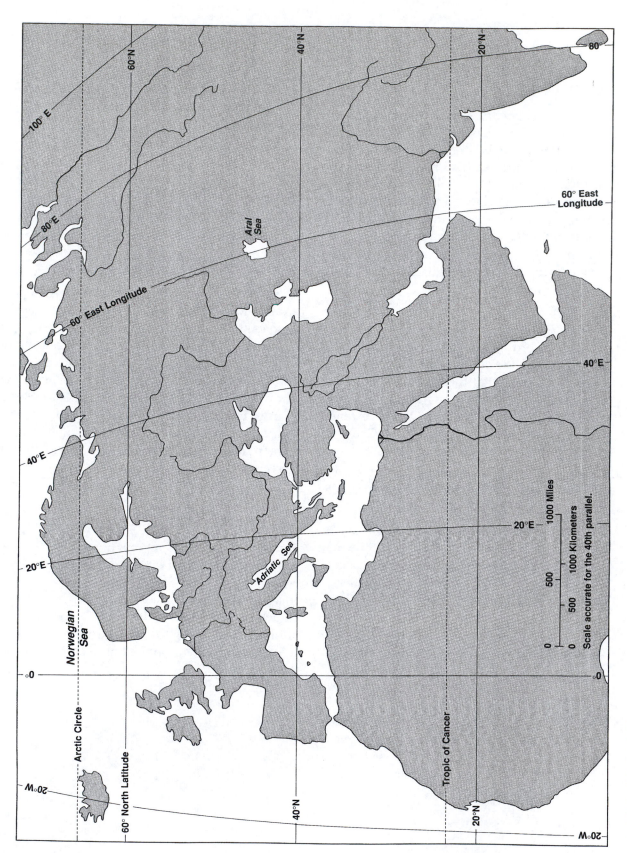

60° East Longitude

60° East Longitude

Aral Sea

Adriatic Sea

Norwegian Sea

1000 Miles

1000 Kilometers

Scale accurate for the 40th parallel.

Arctic Circle

60° North Latitude

Tropic of Cancer

HarperCollins Publishers © 1991

TOPIC 2
Geographic Context: The Ancient Near East

BACKGROUND

Although we often identify Western civilization with Europe, the search for its origins leads to the continents of Asia and Africa. Thus at the beginning students need a map that covers the Mediterranean and Near East. The utility of this map, however, is not confined to the earliest chapters of the story. It will be essential to measure the extent of the empire of Alexander or the reach of Roman governance. One needs a map like this one to understand the nature of the Byzantine culture or the role of the Turkish Empire. The rise of Islam, the crusades, the expansion of Europe, and the power conflicts of modern times are all implicit when a person looks at the map with historical eyes.

PLACES

Label the following on the map:

1. *Oceans*: Atlantic, Indian, Arctic
2. *Seas*: Baltic, North, Mediterranean, Black, Caspian, Red, Arabian
3. *Gulfs*: Persian, Aden, Oman
4. *Islands*: Great Britain, Sri Lanka
5. *Rivers*: Rhine, Danube, Nile, Volga, Euphrates, Indus

WORKING WITH SPACE

1. In the ancient world as well as in modern times canals were constructed across the Isthmus of Suez. The Suez Canal connects the _____ _____ and the _____.
2. In ancient times traders traveled between ports on the Red Sea and the Persian Gulf. Sea-born commerce along this route had to travel around the _____ Peninsula.

3. Locate Mesopotamia on the map. It is the land between the Euphrates and the Tigris rivers. The Fertile Crescent begins at the head of the _____ Gulf and follows the Mesopotamian lands to the northwest. Then it turns to the south, following the eastern shore of the _____ Sea to the other tip of the crescent in the land of _____. Use a colored pen to indicate the Fertile Crescent on your map.

4. Asia Minor is the name given to the extension of Asia that is a peninsula between the _____ , _____ , and _____ seas. Today this land is in the nation of _____ .

5. Note how this map suggests that it was relatively easy to sail from the Persian Gulf to India. Mark that route on the map. Phoenician adventurers sailing west from the Fertile Crescent reached Cornwall in Great Britain and the Canary Islands off of Africa. Mark these routes on your map.

EXTENSIONS

The Mediterranean Sea, the North Sea, and the Baltic Sea served as focal points for key historical developments during various periods of European history. The role of the Indian Ocean is often overlooked, perhaps because it is often cut off on the maps used by students.

Check the index to your textbook and note how often the Indian Ocean appears. Use these references to help develop an outline for a term paper on "The Indian Ocean and Western civilization."

Red Sea

Bosporus

Sea of Marmara

Dardanelles

Ionian Sea

Tyrrhenian Sea

Strait of Gibraltar

500 Miles

500 Kilometers

250

250

0

0

HarperCollins Publishers © 1991

TOPIC 3
Geographic Context: The Mediterranean World

BACKGROUND

David Attenborough, the celebrated zoologist, gave the title, *The First Eden*, to his book on the Mediterranean world. The traditional European location for the Garden of Eden was in the far eastern reaches of the ecumene. Attenborough states that if Paradise must have a precise location, many believe it was much closer, a small, sandy island in the Red Sea. However, Attenborough's choice for Eden is the whole Mediterranean Basin pictured on this map.

This is also the map that is normally used to locate places in classical times and for much of the history of Western civilization through the Middle Ages up to the Renaissance. It certainly has limitations for each of these periods, but these are balanced by the advantage of placing the Mediterranean Sea in the middle of the image, giving it the dominant position and making it the central focus of attention.

PLACES

Label the following on the map:

1. *Ocean:* Atlantic
2. *Seas:* Mediterranean, Red, Black, Adriatic, Aegean
3. *Rivers:* Danube, Rhone, Po, Ebro, Nile
4. *Islands:* Corsica, Sardinia, Sicily, Crete, Cyprus
5. *Mountain Ranges:* Pyrenes, Alps, Appennines

WORKING WITH SPACE

1. Use a red line on the map to mark the route of a traveler by sea who started from Rome and then visited the following places in this order:

a. Naples

b. the site of ancient Carthage

c. Sardinia

d. Marseille

e. Barcelona

f. the Rock of Gibraltar

g. Algiers

2. Use a blue line on the map to trace another voyage, this one starting at Suez on the Gulf of Suez and then proceeding through the _____ _____ to Alexandria, Crete, and Venice. At Venice the party used a train to reach Budapest. Crossing the _____ Peninsula to Istanbul by way of Belgrade, the traveler took a steamer to Crimea for a week's rest. Then she retraced her steps to the Straits, proceeded through the Sea of Marmora and directly across the _____ Sea to_____, the capital city of Greece.

EXTENSIONS

At the end of his book Attenborough raises a question that seems to stick in one's mind when viewing a map of the Mediterranean. He concludes that this is the place where people learned how to conquer the world. Ironically, after the conquest there is danger that everything will be lost in ecological catastrophe. Might this, then, be "the place where we really begin to learn from our mistakes?" (p. 230)

How has the ecology of the Mediterranean world changed due to human activities? How would you go about finding library sources to help you do some research to answer this question? Visit the library and construct a list of five to ten references to consult in doing this research.

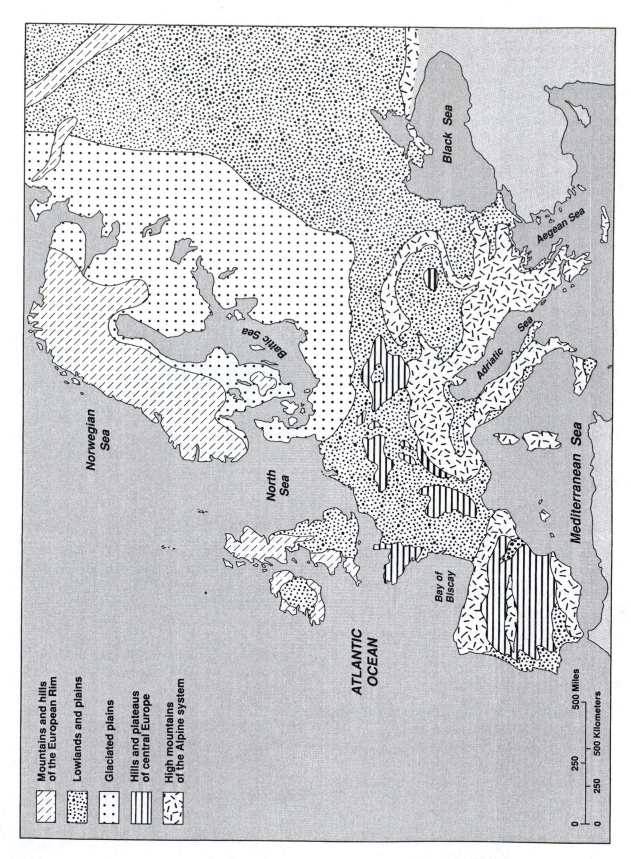

Mountains and hills
of the European Rim

Lowlands and plains

Glaciated plains

Hills and plateaus
of central Europe

High mountains
of the Alpine system

Black Sea

Aegean Sea

Adriatic Sea

Baltic Sea

Norwegian Sea

North Sea

ATLANTIC OCEAN

Bay of Biscay

Mediterranean Sea

0   250   500 Miles

0   250   500 Kilometers

HarperCollins Publishers © 1991

TOPIC 4
Europe's Geographic Context: Landforms

BACKGROUND

A traditional method of analyzing a landscape is to first look at the land surface itself, then to consider the plants that cover it, and then to investigate the structures human activities have placed upon it. The landforms of Europe in a very generalized way fall into a few large categories that extend in irregular bands east and west across the continent.

WORKING WITH SPACE

1. Two upland areas mark the edges of Europe to the north and south. The old mountains and hills of Scandinavia and the British Isles are separated from the younger, higher mountains of the Alpine system in the south by a band of lowlands that stretch from Ireland eastward until they merge with the steppes of Central Asia. Use a shade of brown to color the northern mountains and hills. These cover all of northern and western Scandinavia and a patch that lies inland near the southern tip of this peninsula. The upland region also extends to large areas in the northern and western parts of Great Britain. In Ireland the uplands appear in three coastal sections. Label Scandinavia, Great Britain, and Ireland.

2. Use a shade of orange to color the Alpine system. Begin in Switzerland and note how the mountain system extends without interruption into the Italian and Balkan peninsulas. Crete, northern Sicily, Corsica, and Sardinia are also included in the Alpine system. On the Iberian Peninsula, the system includes three east-west layers, one in the north, one across the center of Spain, and one along the Mediter-ranean coast. Label the Iberian, Italian, and Balkan peninsulas.

3. Various ranges in the Alpine system have names that will appear regularly in the history of Western civilization. Label the Pyrenees, the Alps, the Appennines, and the Carpathians.

4. Use two shades of green to color the great European plain that stretches from central Ireland and southeastern Great Britain eastward across the continent. The line on the map that begins at the Atlantic just south of the Danish Peninsula and extends eastward divides the plain into two sections: the glaciated plains to the north and the mostly nonglaciated lowlands to the south. Lowlands associated with the non-glaciated plain also appear in small patches in Iberia, in the Po Valley plus three more patches along the coast of Italy, and in the southern part of Sicily.

5. Scattered on the great European plain are a variety of hills and plateaus that appear on this map as an archipelago stretching eastward from Normandy. Color these outlying uplands a shade of orange or brown. Label Brittany, the Massif Central in France, and the Sudetes in Poland and Czechoslovakia.

EXTENSIONS

It is instructive to note the locations of Rome and Constantinople, of London and Paris, and of Berlin and Moscow on this map. Write a brief commentary on the geographic locations of these six centers of Western civilization, past and present. Use the map as a reference and write the commentary in the form of an extended caption for the map.

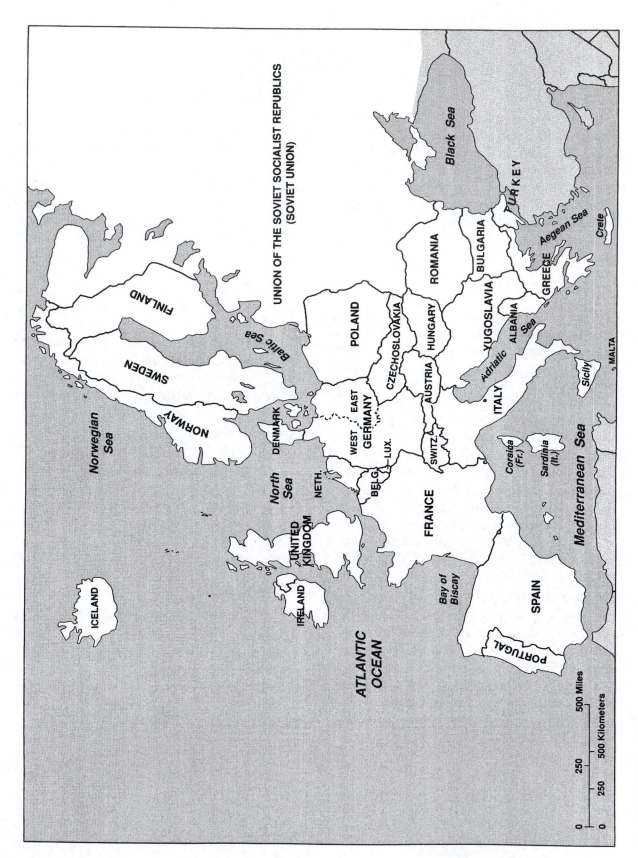

HarperCollins Publishers © 1991

TOPIC 5
Europe's Political Context: Modern Nations

BACKGROUND

Few types of maps show the impress of history as vividly as those that show political boundaries and the names of nation-states. These lines and names are pressed onto a simple physical outline map by the course of historical development. The map is in one sense a demonstration of power. As such there are almost always some areas where the situation is contested and the resolution remains in doubt. Furthermore, a regime may control a region but this fact might not be recognized by other states.

WORKING WITH SPACE

1. Political maps tend to emphasize the geographic size of a nation-state rather than its population, economic status, or political power. Thus the Scandinavian nations of _____ , _____ , and _____ , look imposing on the map but each of these nations has a smaller population than Belgium or the Netherlands. Label Scandinavia and the Low Countries.

2. Parallels and meridians are not used as boundaries in Europe. The European state reflects the historical development of a nationality or a group of associated nationalities. The challenges of combining a democratic polity with a multi-_____ state go a long way toward explaining the dynamic quality of political maps of Europe during the last 150 years. Use a marking pen to trace the western boundaries of the predominantly Slavic nations: Poland, Czechoslovakia, and Yugoslavia. Connect these lines by using the eastern border of Austria, and you will have a rough division between Eastern and Western Europe.

3. The line drawn in number two has been called the shatterbelt of Europe because of the instability of political arrangements and boundaries

in this region. The shatterbelt line extends from the tip of Sweden to the head of the _____ Sea.

4. The mountainous border between France and Spain has endured as a stable boundary region since ancient Roman times. These are the _____ Mountains.

5. The exact legal nature of the Soviet Union has always been something of a puzzle for cartographers. Should the Ukraine, for example, be shown as a separate nation? It is, after all, represented as such in the United Nations. The use of dotted lines to show tentative, qualified, *de facto*, or *de jure* boundaries is always a saving element in drawing political maps.

PLACES

Identify and label on the map the capital cities described below:

1. The largest city in the world north of the 55th parallel is also a capital: _____ .

2. The prime meridian passes through the capital city of _____ .

3. At the beginning of our era, all roads led to this city: _____ .

4. The capital city of continental Europe located farthest west: _____ .

5. The queen city of the Danube, the home of the waltz: _____ .

EXTENSIONS

A handful of very small states that survive in the form of medieval principalities are not labeled on this map. This group would include Liechtenstein, San Marino, Andorra, Vatican City, in addition to Malta. Locate one of these small countries on the map and write a brief essay explaining why it has survived as an independent state.

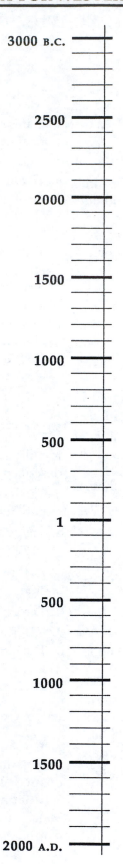

3000 B.C.

2500

2000

1500

1000

500

1

500

1000

1500

2000 A.D.

HarperCollins Publishers © 1991

TOPIC 6
A Chronological Context for Western Civilization

BACKGROUND

There are three steps in developing a chronological context for any historical project, whether it be a survey course in Western civilization, a study of a local community's past, or an autobiography. First, the historian must select certain events as key dates to understand the development of the topic at hand. Next, he or she must list these key events in chronological order. Such a list is called a chronology. The third step is to record these events on a measured timeline such as the one on the opposite page to help develop a periodization scheme for the project.

Periods are created by historians to group events that are similar in character or that seem to be functionally part of the same development. Periods are to time like regions are to space. Both are invented by people to help them understand the things they experience. They don't exist in reality, in the sense that they are mental constructs rather than lines on the ground or special days when trumpets sound at sunrise.

Because periods are mental constructs, each historian is free to develop a periodization scheme that suits his or her perception of reality. Individuals might use different key events and turning points to construct new periods with fresh names. A familiar story like the history of Western civilization has often acquired a standard set of key events, periods, and names that are helpful to have in mind before you proceed with your more detailed study, chapter by chapter and period by period.

WORKING WITH TIME

1. Note how this timeline is set in the middle of the page to help you work with two sets of data. The key events are to be recorded at their precise location in the left-hand column. The space on the right-hand side is for the division of the story into various periods. Start by entering the following on the left-hand side of the page:

c. 3100 B.C.	Sumeria: first writing
c. 2500 B.C.	Great Pyramids
c. 2000 B.C.	Crete: Beginnings of Minoan civilization
c. 1750 B.C.	Hammurabi: Babylonian Empire
c. 1200 B.C.	Jewish exodus from Egypt
753 B.C.	Rome founded (traditional date)
480-335 B.C.	Golden Age of Greece
323 B.C.	Alexander the Great dies
201 B.C.	Rome defeats Carthage
27 B.C.	Roman Empire
330 A.D.	Constantinople established
476 A.D.	Fall of Rome
622 A.D.	*Hegira* of Mohammed
800 A.D.	Charlemagne crowned
1096 A.D.	First Crusade
1215 A.D.	Magna Carta
c. 1500 A.D.	Italian Renaissance
1687 A.D.	Newton's *Principia*
1789 A.D.	French Revolution
1917 A.D.	Russian Revolution
1945 A.D.	World War II ends

2. Now use the right-hand side of the chart to divide the timeline into various periods. One common approach uses the following periodization, but you are free to check the table of contents in your textbook to use an alternative approach.

Early Civilizations	3000 B.C.–500 B.C.
Classical Period	500 B.C. –500 A.D.
Middle Ages	500 A.D.–1500 A.D.
Early Modern Times	1500 A.D.–750 A.D.
Modern Europe	1750 A.D.–1950 A.D.
Contemporary Period	1950 A.D.–

EXTENSIONS

Select one of the events listed on your timeline and write a brief essay explaining why it is considered to be a significant milestone or major turning point in Western civilization.

TOPIC 7
The Dawn of History: Çatal Hüyük, c. 6200 B.C.

BACKGROUND

This wall painting is perhaps the oldest known map. It is also, for modern viewers, one of the most easily understood ancient maps. It is a city plan painted on two walls of a room in a Neolithic community in south-central Anatolia, near what is still the major land route in Turkey between Europe and the Near East. Radio-carbon dating has placed the image at 6200 B.C. ± 100 years. It is a very large figure, nearly nine feet wide, hence only about two-thirds of the image is reproduced here. For a full account see James Mellaart, *Çatal Hüyük: A Neolithic Town in Anatolia* (New York: McGraw-Hill, 1967), from which this drawing is taken.

After archaeologists had uncovered 139 rooms in the complex, they concluded that at least 40 were used for special rites, probably of a religious nature. One of these special rooms, whose walls had often been replastered, contained this large image featuring rows of boxlike shapes. Mellaart was struck by the similarity between the site maps carefully drawn by the archaeologists and the painting on the wall. It was soon apparent that the Neolithic image was a map of the community, or perhaps of the town that immediately preceded the one that the dig was uncovering.

WORKING WITH SPACE

Summarize the information provided below and write your summary on the margins of the map. Draw a box around each explanatory statement and connect the legend with an appropriate spot on the map by means of an arrow. Provide a title for each box.

1. The town site was on a slope with rows of houses or buildings set on graded terraces. The rectangular buildings and the streets set at right angles provided a gridiron look that has characterized much town-planning throughout history.

2. The elongated or linear pattern of the settlement may reflect an orientation to a major road.

3. The large figure beyond the town that looks like a mountain with two peaks is, no doubt, Hasan Dag, a volcano that was active until about 2000 B.C. It supplied the obsidian that was the basis of the settlement's wealth. This glassy volcanic rock was used for making cutting tools, knives, scrapers, weapons, jewelry, ornaments, and a variety of other artifacts.

EXTENSIONS

Consult an atlas of archaeology or some other references about this site and locate some drawings, maps, or photographs to provide more information about it. Include a caption or explanatory notes for each additional graphic image.

HarperCollins Publishers © 1991

TOPIC 8
A Babylonian View of the World

BACKGROUND

The earliest world map still extant is a crude cuneiform tablet from Babylon dating back to at least 500 B.C. and possibly several centuries earlier. Its unfinished quality and the broken condition in which the tablet has survived prevents full scholarly agreement on some aspects of its meaning. It antedates by at least a millennium any world map in the Western tradition.

Because of the crude drawing and the elementary nature of the accompanying text, Eckhard Unger, the scholar who has studied the map most intently, concluded that it was part of a series of tablets that made up an elementary cosmological treatise, something like a school textbook. However, it is a unique map; nothing similar to it has yet been discovered. This raises a question as to whether it represents the view of one particular individual or of the Mesopotamian tradition as a whole. If it is broadly representative—and a schoolbook format would seem to document this—it probably reflects a long-established tradition extending back several more millennia.

The drawing reproduced here that conjecturally completes the map is from Eckhard Unger, "From the Cosmos Picture to the World Map," *Imago Mundi*, II (1937), 1–7.

WORKING WITH SPACE

Use the drawing at the bottom of the page to complete the following activities:

1. The Babylonian cosmos was composed of four basic parts: first, the circle of land that people inhabited; second, a surrounding "Bitter River" or "Earthly Ocean"; third, a series of islands beyond the sea that were transitional regions between the earth and the "Heavenly Ocean"— islands that ordinary people were prevented from visiting; and fourth, the heavens, which were occupied by various constellations and were the abode of the gods. Color each of these cosmic regions a different color. The heavenly realm was presumably represented by another image that would fit on the top of the representation of the earth like a cover over a dish.

2. The map is oriented with northwest on the top, perhaps reflecting the pattern of prevailing winds. Indicate the directions at the side of the image by an arrow pointing north.

3. Two parallel lines such as those extending from the top to the bottom of the image represent rivers in Mesopotamian cartography. In this case it is the Euphrates River. Label the Euphrates River.

4. The rectangle at the center of the map is the city of Babylon where the map was no doubt made. The great city was considered to be at the center of the earth and the cosmos. Label Babylon.

5. The source of the Euphrates is pictured in the mountains at the top of the image. The river flows southward into the great Waterstream Marsh and the Persian Gulf, which is identified as bitter or salt water on the map. Label the mountains and the Persian Gulf.

6. Various cities and kingdoms, marked by circles on the map, extend in the regions around Babylon. Some of these are labeled and some regions are also identified. Label Armenia, Assyria, and Habban.

7. Seven islands are drawn on this reconstruction. Other scholars have suggested that there were six or eight of these semilegendary places. Only four clearly are evident on the unbroken parts of the clay tablet. The island to the north was shrouded in complete darkness. Here the sun was not visible. Provide names for the fragmentary islands suggested on the drawing.

EXTENSIONS

Some modern critics have dismissed this map as crude and inaccurate, documenting a paucity of knowledge and a chauvinistic conceit. Do you agree with this assessment? Develop your response and explain your position in a brief paper.

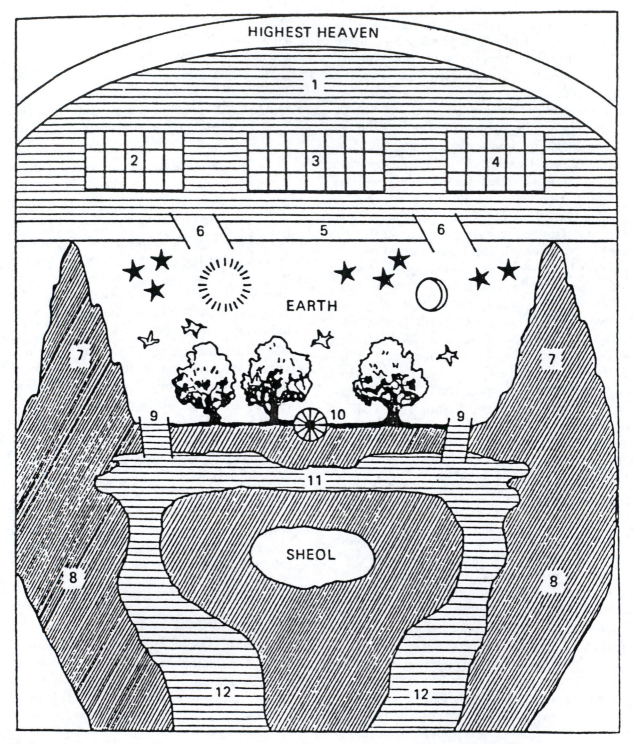

HIGHEST HEAVEN

EARTH

SHEOL

TOPIC 9
A Biblical View of the World

BACKGROUND

The biblical view of the cosmos was not a unique Jewish perspective. The writers of the Old Testament simple adapted the image of the world used by the dominant cultures in the ancient Near East, especially the Mesopotamian empires. As Rabbi Louis Jacobs has pointed out (in *Ancient Cosmologies*, edited by Carmen Blacker and Michael Loewe, 1975), the Jewish preoccupation was not to map the universe but to sing the praises of its creator. They wrote immortal psalms, but any maps they may have made did not endure. Hence a modern drawing is needed to present a cartographic image of the Old Testament world.

The people of ancient times were probably concerned with the vertical structure of the universe, in contrast to the focus on the earth's surface that is characteristic of modern maps. Many of the references to the universe in the Old Testament assume that the reader has a mental image of a cross section of the cosmos. This diagram is from N. M. Sarna's *Understanding Genesis* (New York: Schocken Books, 1966).

WORKING WITH SPACE

1. The basic image parallels the common post-and-lintel construction technique in which a flat surface is supported by posts. The earth itself rests on great pillars. The skies, in turn, are supported by similar columns. However, above the skies the higher heavens had a dome shape, suggesting perhaps another type of structure and another realm of existence. Ancient texts refer to three dimensions of the universe: things on the earth, things above the earth, and things under the earth. Mark these three dimensions on the side of the illustration.

2. Sheol is a biblical name for "the nether world" but it also is used as a synonym for death, the grave, or hell. The idea that punishment takes place in Sheol is a latter addition from Hellenistic times. In the original sense it was a place of waiting where people who had died slept in a state of nothingness. Find a biblical reference to Sheol and write the passage on a note card.

3. The Great Flood was caused by an outpouring from the _____ of the deep as well as the opening of the _____ of heaven (Genesis 7:11).

4. The three chambers above the firmament are for (2) snow, (3) hail, and (4) the winds. Label them.

PLACES

Record the appropriate numbers for the part of the biblical view of the word in each space below.

_____ 1. Pillars of the earth

_____ 2. Pillars of the sky

_____ 3. Navel of the earth

_____ 4. Waters under the earth

_____ 5. Rivers of the deep

_____ 6. The firmament

_____ 7. Fountains from the deep

_____ 8. Waters above the firmament

_____ 9. Windows of heaven

EXTENSIONS

Find a passage in the Bible that describes the universe or a part of it. Use the diagram to explain the text in a paragraph or two of commentary.

HarperCollins Publishers © 1991

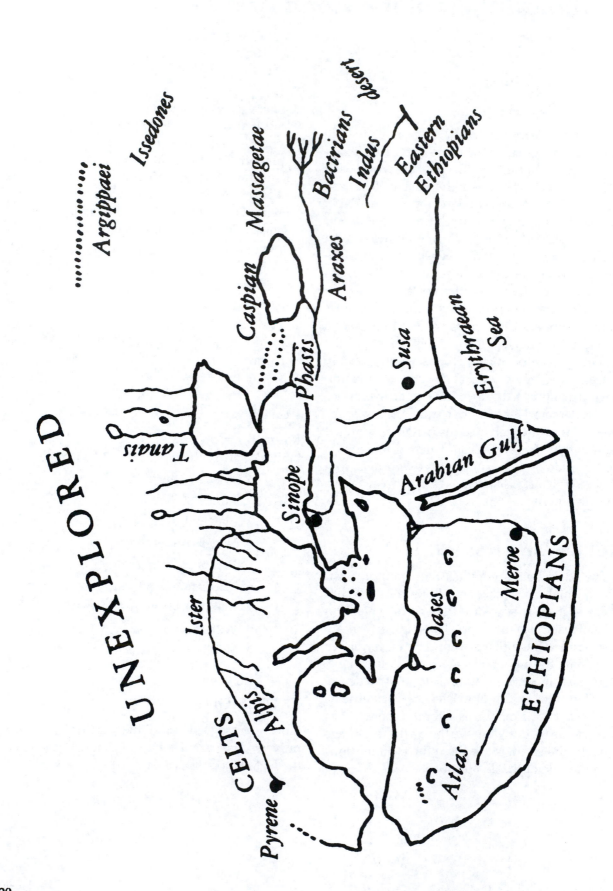

TOPIC 10
Herodotus: A Reconstruction of his World

BACKGROUND

The development of cartography in the Greek world was deeply influenced by two currents that seemed to clash against one another. The contesting streams provoked disagreements about the nature of the earth and these, in turn, stimulated further investigation and theorizing. The first current was the traditional view of the universe largely shaped by the Mesopotamian tradition. The second was the spirit of rational inquiry that was a hallmark of Greek culture.

Herodotus, who had traveled extensively on three continents, expressed his amusement at those who followed the traditional view: "For my part, I cannot but laugh when I see numbers of persons drawing maps of the world without having any reason to guide them; making, as they do, the ocean-stream to run all round the earth, and the earth itself to be an exact circle, as if described by a pair of compasses."

Like many classical writers, Herodotus preferred to tell about the earth in words rather than maps. No contemporary map apparently accompanied his writings; at least none has survived. This reconstruction of his world view is from O. A. W. Dilke's *Greek and Roman Maps* (1985).

WORKING WITH SPACE

1. Note how this reconstruction sets no outer bounds to the ecumene, except in Africa. Instead it starts with the Mediterranean region, which Herodotus considered his home, and works outward from this base. Label Africa, Asia, and Europe on this map.

2. The Erythraean Sea (or Indian Ocean) balances the Mediterranean and provides a focus for civilizations in the East. Note how the Arabian Gulf reaches up to almost connect the two great seas. Several canals were built in the ancient world to make this connection. Label the Indian Ocean and the Mediterranean Sea.

3. The great length of the Nile impressed most cartographers, and they often turned it to the east or west to accommodate its length in their restricted view of Africa's size. They may also have confused the headwaters of the Niger and the Nile. Label the Nile River.

4. Herodotus and the ancient Greeks had a much more detailed knowledge of Central Asia than they did of Western Europe. Herodotus knew Bactria and the Indus Valley. However, Britain was off the map. Draw in Great Britain on the map.

5. The Ister River, or the Danube, was exaggerated in its length like the Nile. It does reach behind the Alps, but not as far as pictured here. Label the Danube River. Note the symmetry of the Danube and Nile rivers.

PLACES

Find these places on the map:

_____	1. City on the upper Nile
_____	2. Capital of Persia
_____	3. People living north of the Danube
_____	4. City of Asia Minor
_____	5. People living between the Araxes and Indus river

EXTENSIONS

This reconstruction emphasized aids to travelers. Some followed river courses, some went from oasis to oasis across the desert, and some used islands to sail the sea. Draw routes for hypothetical journeys on the map using these aids to travel and navigation. Then write a letter describing the trip as it might have been taken in 450 B.C.

HarperCollins Publishers © 1991

TOPIC 11
Ptolemy: A World Map of the Second Century A.D.

BACKGROUND

Claudius Ptolemy is one of the most celebrated names in the history of cartography. Writing in Alexandria in the second century A.D., his books summed up the achievements of Hellenistic science and became the chief conduit for this wisdom to reach Western civilization in the Renaissance. Although much of his work and the tradition it represented were almost totally forgotten in Western Europe during the so-called "Dark Ages," they were kept alive in the Islamic world and in the libraries of Byzantine scholars.

Greek scholars brought Ptolemy's geographic texts to the West in the early 15th century and soon translated them into Latin. Widely circulated in various manuscripts, Ptolemy's work was printed in many editions, most of them accompanied by a series of maps that became the first printed atlas. The map reproduced here is from the Rome edition of the *Geographia* published in 1478 A.D

WORKING WITH SPACE

1. Ptolemy advocated a scientific or inductive approach to cartography. He established a grid made up of parallels and meridians much like we use today. He then advocated determining the latitude and longitude for specific places on the basis of astronomical observations and actual measurement. Most of his book was a list of places and their coordinates. Once these were placed on the grid, a map could be sketched on the basis of established points. Use a colored pen to highlight the equator on this map.

2. North is at the top on Ptolemaic maps and west is to the left. Ptolemy began with a prime meridian at the farthest observed place to the west, in the Canary Islands. Use a colored pen to highlight the Canary or Fortunate Islands.

3. The distance around the earth was given as 360 degrees, but the ecumene occupied only one–fourth of the globe. Use a colored pen to highlight the scales of longitude at the top and the bottom of the map. Mark the 90th meridian at the center of Ptolemy's map. What three bodies of water did it cross?

a. _____

b. _____

c. _____

4. The fabled island of Taprobana dominated the Indian Ocean. The Indian subcontinent was "flattened" and is therefore difficult to locate. Both the Indus and the Ganges rivers appear on the map. Use a colored pen to highlight Taprobana, later known as Ceylon or Sri Lanka.

5. In Africa the Nile River was pictured with a high degree of accuracy. Use a colored pen to highlight the Nile River and its tributaries.

PLACES

Use the map to find these places:

1. The largest island in the Indian Ocean.

   _____

2. Ptolemy's name for the Canary Islands.

   _____

3. The body of water at the very center of Ptolemy's map. _____

4. The end of Ptolemy's world in the northwest.

   _____

5. The lands bordering the Indian Ocean on the south. _____

EXTENSIONS

It has been observed that the rediscovery of Ptolemy's map seized the minds of 15th-century scholars with much greater force than the discovery of a new world by Columbus and his colleagues. Why would this be so? How can you explain it? Develop your answer in a paragraph or two.

HarperCollins Publishers ©1991

2000 B.C.

1750

1500

1250

1000

750

500

250

1

250

500 A.D.

HarperCollins Publishers © 1991

TOPIC 12
Ancient History: A Chronological Context

BACKGROUND

One of the most difficult challenges in studying the ancient world is to connect events happening in a variety of different regions. At a minimum, students need to relate developments in Mesopotamia, Egypt, Greece, and Rome. To connect events or developments happening in the same year is to use the synchronic dimension of time; to synchronize means to group things that share the same time. Another dimension of time, the diachronic, emphasizes the way things are connected in the passage of time.

Although the timeline developed in this activity might suggest some diachronic elements, its major purpose is to help visualize the contemporary aspects of developments in the Near East, North Africa, Greece, and Rome.

WORKING WITH TIME

1. Begin by assigning a title to each side of the timeline. Use "Near East and North Africa" for the left-land column and "Greece and Rome" for the one on the right-hand side.

2. Note that the timeline begins in 2000 B.C. and uses 50 years as the interval between each mark. This represents about one lifetime in the ancient world, or about two generations. Civilization was 1000 years old in Mesopotamia and Egypt in the year 2000 B.C. Note this fact on the timeline.

3. Enter the following events in the Near East-North Africa column:

c. 1750 B.C.	Hammurabi and Babylonian Empire
1567 B.C.	New Kingdom in Egypt
c. 1200 B.C.	Jewish exodus from Egypt
c. 1000 B.C.	Phoenician alphabet developed
814 B.C.	Traditional founding of Carthage

721–612 B.C.	Assyrian Empire
550 B.C.	Rise of Persia
332–329 B.C.	Alexander's conquests
290 B.C.	Library founded at Alexandria
30 A.D.	Death of Cleopatra; Egypt becomes a Roman province
116 A.D.	Rome completes conquest of Mesopotamia
224 A.D.	Rise of Sasanian dynasty in Persia
429 A.D.	Vandal kingdom in North Africa

4. Enter the following events under the Greece and Rome column:

c. 2000–1450 B.C.	Minoan Civilization on Crete
c. 1600–1200 B.C.	Mycanaean Civilization
776 B.C.	First Olympic games
753 B.C.	Traditional founding of Rome
490–480 B.C.	Persian Wars
480–338 B.C.	Golden Age of Greece
338 B.C.	Macedonian conquest of Greece
241–146 B.C.	Punic Wars
146 B.C.	Roman conquest of Greece
49 B.C.	Caesar conquers Gaul
27 B.C.	Roman Empire established
313 A.D.	Edict of Milan
330 A.D.	Constantinople founded
476 A.D.	Fall of Roman Empire in the West
486 A.D.	Clovis establishes Frankish Kingdom

EXTENSIONS

Make a list of connections between the two columns. Make at least five statements.

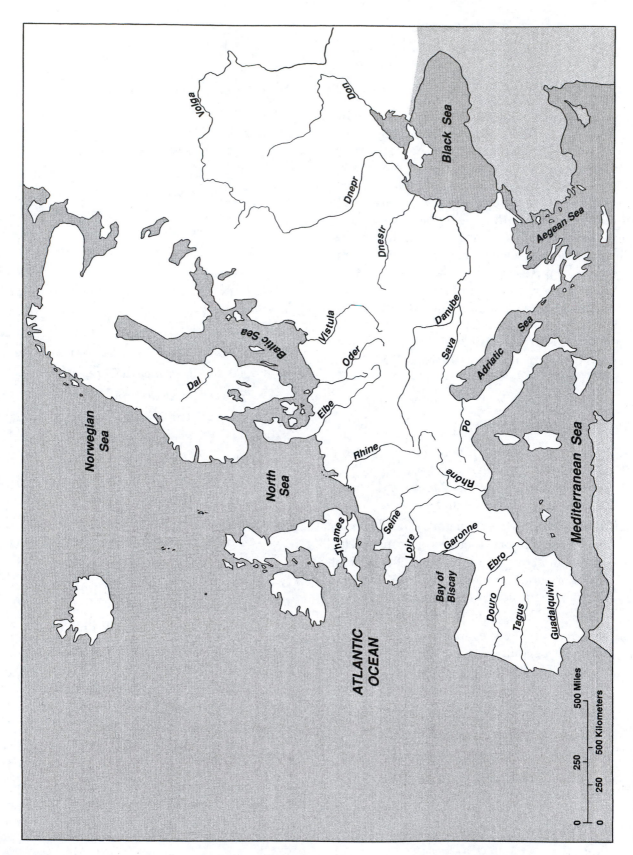

HarperCollins Publishers © 1991

TOPIC 13
The Medieval World: A Geographic Context

BACKGROUND

The base map used for this activity focuses on the rivers of Europe, because they served as main routes for communication as well as the movement of goods and people in medieval times. The map also shifts attention north from the Mediterranean basin to include the full extent of northern Europe. This is necessary to show the lands of the Vikings, but it carries with it a significant limitation. The Mediterranean continued to be a pivotal region in almost every respect throughout the Middle Ages. One map is seldom sufficient to illustrate all the historical forces at work in any event or period.

PLACES

As you locate these places and record them on the outline map, note how they are grouped by regions based largely on seas and river basins.

1. *Mediterranean Region:* Antioch in Syria, Constantinople, Venice, Rome, Florence, Milan, Genoa, Marseilles, Barcelona, Granada
2. *Danube Basin:* Vienna, Budapest, Augsburg
3. *Rhine–Rhone corridor:* Strasbourg, Cologne, Lyon
4. *Baltic and North Seas:* Hamburg, Lübeck, Danzig, Stockholm, Bergen.
5. *English Channel–Lowlands Area:* London, Paris, Antwerp
6. *Inland Centers:* Novgorod, Kiev, Cracow, Prague, Toledo

WORKING WITH SPACE

1. Use a marking pen to show the Muslim advances into Europe: first across the Strait of Gibraltar, into Spain and France; second through Asia Minor, to Constantinople, and eventually up the Danube to Vienna.

2. The Viking invasions all began on the coasts of Scandinavia. Use a marking pen to trace these routes:

   (A) from Norway to Iceland, Ireland, and along the Atlantic coast from Bordeaux southward into the Mediterranean as far as Sicily.

   (B) Another sea route began in the Danish straits and reached toward London and Paris.

   (C) A third major route crossed the Baltic Sea from Sweden and reached Novgorod, then proceeded southward to Kiev and the Black Sea.

3. The Magyar Invasions of the ninth century began along the northern coast of the Black Sea and extended up the Danube, branching north and south of the Alps and eventually reaching the Rhine, Rhone, and Po valleys. Mark this route with a pen.

EXTENSIONS

Select any one of the towns listed on the map and develop an outline for a paper on its history during the Middle Ages. Write the introductory paragraph for this paper.

HarperCollins Publishers © 1991

europa & affrica

De. Asia & eius partibus

A sia ex noie cuiusdã mu/ lieris est ap/ pellata. que apud anti/ quos imperiu orientis tenuit. Hec in tercia or bis parte disposita. ab oriente ortu solis. a me ridie oceáo. ab occidůo nostro mari finitur. a septentrione meothide lacu & tanai fluuio ter minatur. Habet autem prouincias multas et re giones. quarũ breuiter nomina et situs expediam. sumpto initio a paradiso. Paradisus est locus in orientis partibus constitu/

Meridies

MARE

ASIA ·
Sem

Mare magnum siue
mediter
raneum

AFRICA
Cham

EVROPA
Iafeth

Oriens

Occidens

Septentrio

HarperCollins Publishers © 1991

TOPIC 14
Isidore of Seville: A T-O Map

BACKGROUND

Isidore was Bishop of Seville when he compiled an encyclopedia of knowledge about 630 A.D. The work was really a compilation of compilations, using as its sources similar works summing up the knowledge of classical authors and the teachings of the church fathers. Books XIII and XIV dealt with geography, and a T-O map became a regular feature in this section. The encyclopedia was usually called *Origins* or *Etymologae* because of Isidore's interest in explaining the origin of words. The work was more remarkable for the scope of its contents than the depth of its thought. It remained a popular work up to the end of the Renaissance.

The T-O maps became simple diagrams of how the earth was arranged according to Christian concepts. They were meant to provide a general view of the world rather than to delineate the shape of continents or actual distances and directions. The image of the cross made them theological or devotional statements as well. In the Middle Ages everything had an allegorical significance as a type for eternal verities. The general image on the map, however, carried on a long tradition of visualizing the earth that antedated Christianity.

WORKING WITH SPACE

1. The map is "oriented" to the direction of the rising sun, an ancient tradition. In the Christian view, Paradise was located in the Far East. Draw a direction indicator at the side of the image with an arrow pointing to the east.

2. The cardinal directions are given in Latin at the four sides of the image. What name is used for:

   _____ **a.** the rising sun

   _____ **b.** the setting sun

   _____ **c.** the midday sun

   _____ **d.** the seven stars
    (of Ursa Major)

3. The idea of a protean ocean from which the land arose is a common theme in many mythic traditions. The biblical stories of creation and the flood relate to this idea. Note how the encircling waters in this map are divided from the seas and rivers that form the "T" between the continents. The Latin phrase for the ocean sea is

   _____.

4. The continents are labeled according to the classical nomenclature. Each one is then assigned to one of the sons of Noah according to the division of the world in Genesis. Shem (Sem), the oldest son, received the larger birthright portion in _____ . Ham (Cham) and Jafeth received _____ and _____ , respectively.

5. The "T" of the map was formed by rivers and seas. The stem, labeled "Mediterranean" is self-explanatory. The crossbar was formed by waters stretching from the Don or Danube river through the Black, Aegean, and Mediterranean seas and then up the Nile River. Label the Black Sea and the Nile River on the map.

EXTENSIONS

If a reader were to elaborate Isidore's map in the mind's eye, he or she could visualize Paradise at the top of the map, Jerusalem in the center, and the Pillars of Hercules at the bottom. Find another map made during the Middle Ages such as the one used as the basis for Topic 17. Look for these same three features and write a brief commentary explaining how Isidore's diagram helps to explain other medieval world maps.

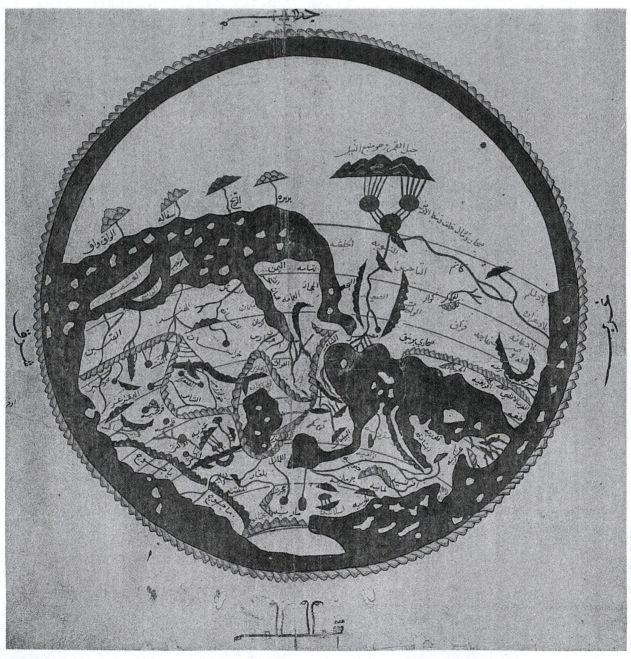

TOPIC 15
Al-Idrisi: Map of the World, 1154 A.D.

BACKGROUND

Ash-Sharif al-Idrisi was born at Ceuta across the Strait of Gibraltar from Europe. Educated in Muslim Spain, at Cordoba, he became a world traveler, traversing not only the length of the Mediterranean world, but visiting England, France and perhaps even Central Asia as well. His writings attracted a deal of attention and he was called in 1138 to come to Sicily where the Norman king Roger II wanted to establish a geographic institute. Al-Idrisi spent the next 22 years of his life as the "executive director" of a group of scholars dedicated to the task of compiling the geographic knowledge then available.

The sources used by the Sicilian geographers started with Ptolemy (see Topic 11) and extended to Muslim itineraries, travel accounts, sea charts, and historical compilations. Roger II actively participated in the research, modeling his kingship on the sultanships of North Africa rather than the crusading kingdoms of Europe. Although a Christian, he lived in the oriental style complete with a harem and a center for Muslim scholars.

After 15 years of research al-Idrisi presented a summary of his findings to his patron in a geographic compendium entitled "The Delight of One who Wishes to Traverse the Regions of the World." Several versions of this Arabic text survived under the short title of *Roger's Book*. The map reproduced here is from a manuscript in Oxford, which is a copy of a shortened version of the compendium al-Idrisi made for Roger's son William, called "The Garden of Joys." It includes 70 regional maps in addition to this circular map.

WORKING WITH SPACE

1. Note that the map looks "upside down" because Arabic maps are oriented with south on the top and west to the right. The cardinal directions are given at the edges of the map. Draw a directional symbol in one corner of the page with an arrow pointing to the north.

2. The curved parallels divide the ecumene into seven climates or regions, following the practice of the Hellenistic cartographers, especially Ptolemy (see Topic 11). Use a marking pen to highlight the equator. Label it.

3. It was not common Islamic practice to divide the earth into continents. Arabia is at the center of a unified ecumene. Note how the Mediterranean Sea and the Indian Ocean balance one another. Color and label Arabia.

4. The Nile River is joined to parts of the Niger and Senegal rivers to produce one riverine system in Africa. Africa itself has a huge extension eastward. Label the Nile, Niger, and Senegal rivers.

5. There are many islands in the Indian Ocean. The portrayal of this region varies greatly in the various surviving manuscripts of al-Idrisi. Label the Indian Ocean.

PLACES

Locate the following places on the map by placing the numbers on the map in the correct location.

1. Black Sea
2. Caspian Sea
3. Italy
4. Sicily
5. Ceuta
6. Cordoba
7. Cairo
8. Jerusalem
9. Mecca
10. Constantinople

EXTENSIONS

How would you go about finding additional information on Al-Idrisi or Roger II's Norman kingdom in Sicily? Visit the library and find five to ten bibliographic references that might be useful. Make a bibliography card for each one. Then find one of the references and write a paragraph summarizing its contents and evaluating its usefulness.

HarperCollins Publishers © 1991

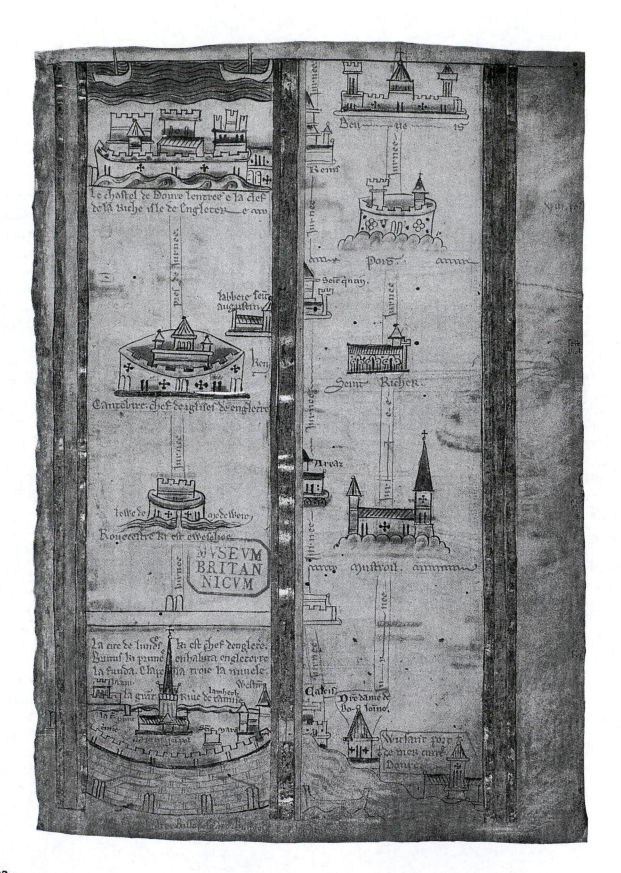

HarperCollins Publishers © 1991

TOPIC 16
Matthew Paris: Itinerary Map of 1253 A.D.

BACKGROUND

Matthew Paris became a monk at St. Albans in Britain in 1217. His name probably refers to his place of birth or the city where he received his education. In addition to continuing a celebrated *Chronicle*, he wrote lives of the saints, several biographies, and a variety of other pieces. He also was an artist and a cartographer.

His "Itineraries," or set of road maps, showed the route from London to south Italy. An inscription on one version indicated the reason for the elaborate production: "Earl Richard, brother of the king of England, was offered the crown of all this country [Apulia]. . . . This was in the time of Pope Innocent IV, who made him the offer in the year of grace 1253."

WORKING WITH SPACE

1. This type of map is called a strip map. It shows only a narrow strip of land along a route. In this case two separate parts of the map are drawn side by side. The itinerary begins at the lower left and follows the road up the map on the left–hand side. The route continues on the second panel on the lower right and then proceeds up this panel in similar fashion. Use blue to color the water at the top of the left panel and at the bottom of the right panel. Label the water as the English Channel or the Straits of Dover.

2. The route begins in London, shown as a large walled city on the map. A spire dominates the cityscape. Label London.

3. The road on the left–hand part of the map leads from London to Dover Castle on the English Channel. Along the way it passes through Canterbury with its cathedral still under construction. Label Canterbury and Dover Castle.

4. Note the boats that seem to be waiting by the English shore to take travelers and pilgrims across the channel. At Calais, after crossing the straits, two routes are given on the map. The one on the left leads through Arras to Reims. The alternative road takes a swing to the south toward Paris. Label the road to Paris.

5. Beuveis (Beauvais) at the top of the map is only about 40 miles from the center of Paris. Here builders pushed gothic vaulting beyond its limits, the cathedral collapsed, and it had to be rebuilt.

EXTENSIONS

The notations on the roads between major villages and towns indicate the distances between them, usually in terms of the number of days needed for the journey. A contemporary source calculated that once a pilgrim arrived in Rome, a journey of only 1425 more days would take him or her all the way across the ecumene to the gates of paradise.

Write a letter of advice from Matthew Paris to a pilgrim contemplating such a journey to Paradise. Include a map for the last leg of the journey if you wish.

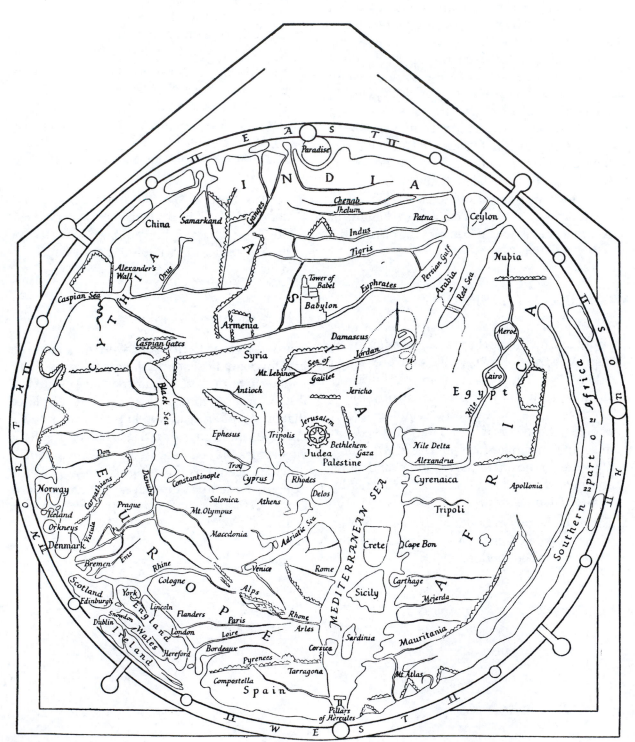

TOPIC 17
The Hereford Map, c. 1285 A.D.: A Key

BACKGROUND

The great medieval map at Hereford Cathedral in Britain has been called the preeminent world map of the High Middle Ages. It exhibits almost all the features of late *mappaemundi* and does so on such a large scale and with such a wealth of detail that close study of the map serves as a stimulating introduction to medieval culture. The map is drawn on a large single skin of vellum measuring 54 x 64 inches. It may have been used as an altarpiece in a chapel at one time, but little is recorded about its early history.

As a summary of late medieval geographic thought, the Hereford Map provides an excellent window to a world we have lost. Two scholars, W. L. Bevan and H. W. Phillott, prepared this sketch to serve as a guide for their detailed study of the map, *Medieval Geography*, first published in 1873.

WORKING WITH SPACE

1. Vellum is made from the hide of an ox. A piece of vellum was cut so that it was nearly square in shape, with a trapezoidal extension using the skin of the animal's neck. The island located in the far east, on the neck portion of the vellum is _____.

2. The ecumene is represented by a circle surrounded by the bitter ocean very much like the Mesopotamian world map or the diagram of Isidore of Sevelle (See Topics 8 and 14). The _____ are located where the Mediterranean Sea meets the Bitter Ocean.

3. The ecumene is divided into three continents by the familiar "T" of waters that occupy the lower half of the circle of lands. The Mediterranean Sea extends from the Pillars of Hercules pictured at the bottom to the city of _____, which occupies the place of honor at the center of the map.

4. Babylon with its Tower of Babel seems to be a major competitor with the Holy City. The map represents this world struggling between good and evil, not in redemption as the City of God. Babylon is located on the _____ River.

5. The Caspian Sea is presented as an inlet of the ocean. It also receives the waters of the _____ River in the vicinity of Alexander's Wall.

PLACES

Study the map and check whether or not these geographic facts are correctly indicated on the Hereford Map. Answer yes or no.

_____ 1. Constantinople is located near the entrance to the Black Sea.

_____ 2. The Atlas Mountains are located in the northwestern part of Africa.

_____ 3. Scotland is on the same island as England and Wales.

_____ 4. Ceylon is east of India.

_____ 5. The Jordan River flows out of the Sea of Galilee.

EXTENSIONS

In 1989 officials of the Hereford Cathedral raised the possibility of selling their famous map. Should the map be kept in the cathedral or placed in a museum or library, possibly in another country? Write a letter arguing for one side or another of this issue. Use as many points as you can to support your position.

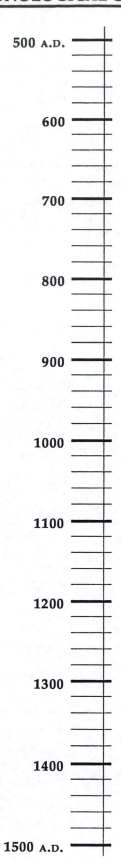

500 A.D.

600

700

800

900

1000

1100

1200

1300

1400

1500 A.D.

TOPIC 18
Medieval History: A Chronological Context

BACKGROUND

The Middle Ages in Western civilization are often divided into three parts. The Early Middle Ages begin about 500 A.D. when the center of the Roman Empire had shifted to Constantinople and imperial control disintegrated in the West. The onslaught of barbarian invasions, the rise of Islam in the century between Muhammad's flight from Mecca to the Battle of Poitiers in France (622–732), and the Viking expansion beginning about 793 characterized the early period as one of instability.

By the year 1000 Western Europe had reached a level of stability that permitted a more orderly development of society and culture. This era, 1000–1300 A.D., is sometimes called the High Middle Ages. It was the age of the crusades (1096–1204) and of Gothic cathedrals (Chartres was begun in 1154).

After 1300 A.D. Western society was hit by a series of crises—a great famine in 1315–1317, the ravages of the Black Death in 1347–1350, and the Great Schism in the Western church, 1378–1417. In the 15th century, by the time of the fall of Constantinople to the Turks in 1453, new currents were sweeping Europe into the Renaissance, the Age of Discovery, and the Reformation. The date 1500 is often used to mark the end of the Middle Ages.

WORKING WITH TIME

1. Draw lines across the timeline to divide the Middle Ages into three sections: early, high, and late.

2. Record the events listed in the Background section on the left-hand side of the chart.

3. Some additional major events are listed below. Add these to the left-hand side of your chart:

800 A.D.	Charlemagne crowed
1066 A.D.	Norman conquest of England
1215 A.D.	Magna Charta
1429 A.D.	Joan of Arc's vision

4. Now use the right-hand side of the chart to indicate the lifespan of the following medieval people:

Justinian	482–565
Muhammad	570–632
Charlemagne	768–814
Francis of Assisi	1181–1226
Aquinas	1225–1274
Dante	1265–1321
Chaucer	1340–1400

EXTENSIONS

Use your textbook to add some information to the timeline. Note how the material is organized by period or by topic. Use one of the blank timelines in the appendix to trace the development of one or two topics in medieval life. For example, architecture could be listed on one side and literature on the other.

TOPIC 19
Map of America, 1540 A.D.

BACKGROUND

This map of the New World was published by Sebastian Münster as part of an edition of Ptolemy's geography issued in Basel in 1540. It is one of the earliest general maps of the Americas and reveals a knowledge of both the eastern and western sides of the continents. The north Pacific is the only large portion of the map drawn mainly from conjecture. The map testifies to Münster's geographical knowledge as well as to his skill as a cartographer. It also reveals the extent of European knowledge of the newfound world less than 50 years after the landfall of Columbus in 1492.

PLACES

In order to clarify various aspects of the map, label the following places:

1. Atlantic Ocean (*Oceanus occidentalis* and *Sinus Atlanticus*)
2. Pacific Ocean (*Mare pacificum*)
3. Spain (*Hispania*)
4. Ireland (*Hiberia*)
5. Canary Islands (*Fortunatae ins.*)
6. Strait of Magellan
7. Japan (*Zipangri*)
8. Florida
9. China (*Cathay* and *India superior*)
10. Hudson Bay (apparently a lucky guess by Münster)
11. Rio de la Plata
12. Amazon River

WORKING WITH SPACE

1. The map of the New World of 1540 indicates the provisions of the Treaty of _____ in 1494 by picturing the flag of _____ on the island later known as _____ and the flag of _____ in the south Atlantic Ocean.

2. Brazil is labeled as the land of the _____ and a vivid illustration shows various body parts ready to be roasted over a fire.

3. The North Pacific is filled with an archipelago of _____ islands, the largest of which is _____ , known today as _____ .

4. The two largest islands in the West Indies have the same names today as in 1540. They are _____ and _____ .

5. The islands in the middle of the Pacific Ocean are the uninhabited Disappointment Islands that _____ reached in January, 1521. The ship drawn on the map is the *Victoria*, his flagship.

EXTENSIONS

Choose one of the following explorers and write a brief description of his voyage(s). Use this map as an essential part of your narrative.

Columbus

Magellan

Cabot

Vespucci

Verrazano

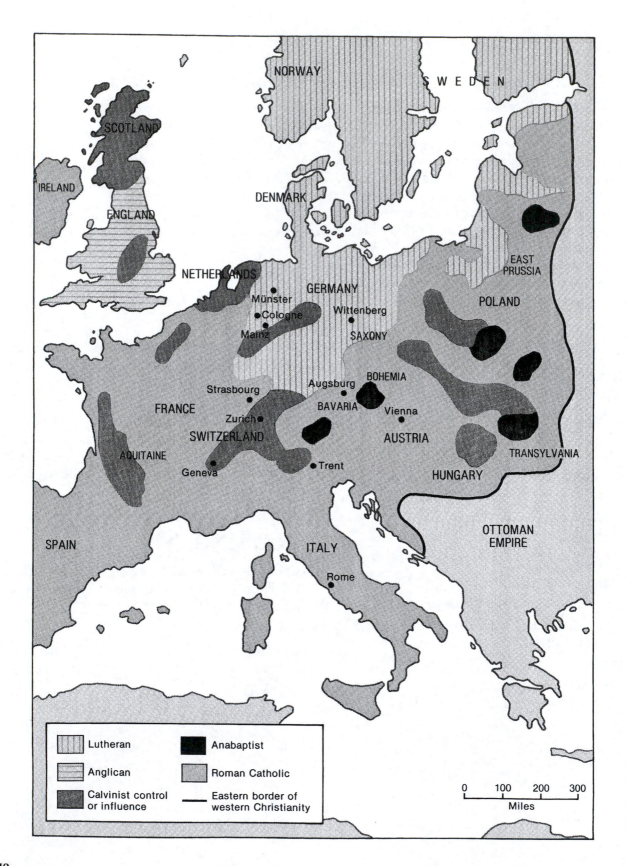

NORWAY

SWEDEN

SCOTLAND

IRELAND

ENGLAND

DENMARK

NETHERLANDS

GERMANY

EAST PRUSSIA

POLAND

Münster

Cologne

Wittenberg

Mainz

SAXONY

Strasbourg

Augsburg

BOHEMIA

FRANCE

Zurich

BAVARIA

Vienna

SWITZERLAND

AUSTRIA

AQUITAINE

TRANSYLVANIA

Geneva

Trent

HUNGARY

SPAIN

ITALY

OTTOMAN EMPIRE

Rome

	Lutheran		Anabaptist
	Anglican		Roman Catholic
	Calvinist control or influence	—	Eastern border of western Christianity

0   100   200   300

Miles

HarperCollins Publishers © 1991

TOPIC 20
The Division of Christianity, c. 1550 A.D.

BACKGROUND

Martin Luther ended one of his hymns with the prayer, "Give your Church, Lord, to see; Days of peace and unity. O Lord, have mercy!" The reform movement that grew out of Luther's teaching, however, soon unleashed forces that fractured the world of the medieval church beyond repair. A map of European religion in 1550 A.D., four years after Luther's death, thus carries the title, "The Division of Christianity."

WORKING WITH SPACE

1. The major religious difference on this map is the division of the Mediterranean Basin between the Christian and Moslem religions. In 1550 almost the entire population along the southern shores of the Mediterranean Sea followed Islam. Label this region "Islam."

2. The second major religious division indicated on the map separates the Western and the Eastern branches of Christianity. The Eastern Orthodox Church in general used the Greek language and looked to the Patriarch of Constantinople for leadership. Western or Latin Christianity, up to the time of Luther, centered on the Pope at Rome. Use a pen to highlight the general border between Eastern and Western Christianity.

3. Note that Christian peoples in the Balkan region were subject to the Islamic empire of the Ottoman Turks. In some of these provinces Islam gained a strong following, and especially in Albania, which today remains a largely Islamic nation in Europe. Label Albania on the map.

4. Before Luther various regions in central Europe had seen popular expressions of religious dissatisfaction. John Huss, a precursor of the Reformation in Bohemia, was burned at the stake as a heretic in 1415. A rebellion followed that ended only when Bohemia received special concessions that later made it a center for the Anabaptist movement. Circle Bohemia on the map.

5. The Reformation may be dated from 1517 when Martin Luther, a young monk at Wittenberg, raised a series of issues for debate in 95 theses or statements. Instead of debate the issues soon led to schism when various German princes protected Luther and became protestors or Protestants. Circle Wittenberg on the map.

6. Lutheranism soon spread throughout northern Germany and into Scandinavia. Color the Lutheran areas on the map.

7. John Calvin followed Luther as a protestant but developed a much different theological approach in his *Institutes of the Christian Religion* (1536). From a base in Geneva, Calvin's theology gained a widespread following in parts of Germany, France, the Low Countries, the British Isles, and Eastern Europe. Circle Geneva and color these Calvinist regions.

8. Use a third color to shade the regions that remained loyal to the Pope at Rome. Note that most regions south of the Alps and the Pyrenees remained solidly Roman Catholic, although the church also changed a good deal in responding to the reform movements in the north.

9. The Church of England represented a special case because it achieved an independent status as much for political as for religious reasons. Great Britain had large numbers of Calvinist and Roman Catholic adherents, but in the end most people supported a moderate position in a national Anglican church. In Scotland, however, the church became Presbyterian, following a Calvinist tradition.

EXTENSIONS

Augsburg and Trent, cities on either side of the Alps, became sites where the basic beliefs of Lutheranism and Roman Catholicism were written down. Write a brief paper on the Augsburg Confession (1530) or the Council of Trent (1545–63) and use this map in the course of your essay.

HarperCollins Publishers © 1991

NOVA ET AUCTA ORBIS TERRAE DESCRIPTIO AD USUM NA

vigantium emendate accommodata

(Prester John)

Oceanus Scythicus

Mongul

Cathay

Thebet

Indostan

A S I A

Sibier

Mare

Rubrum

Java minor

30

60

(Diagram of courses)

Groenlant

270

360

90

EUROPA

Libya

AFRICA

(Note on Ganges)

Pars continentis australis

Oceanus

Aethiopicus

Brasilia

Patagones

Terra del Fuego

N.caribana

A V O N

Mare estis dulcium

N O V A

F R A N C I A

Apalchen

I N D I A

Hispania Nova

La California

El Streto de Anian

Asia Extremum

(Dedication)

(Explanation of projection)

Guinea Nova

(Measuring distances)

Map of North Polar Region

30

30

60

HarperCollins Publishers © 1991

TOPIC 21
Mercator's Map, 1569 A.D.

BACKGROUND

Gerhard Mercator (1512–94) is probably the most celebrated cartographer in the history of Western civilization. He was foremost in emphasizing the scientific rather than the artistic dimension in the making of maps. His most famous map, which is outlined here, appeared in 1569. Similar sheets covering the whole world can still be purchased today in many drugstores or office supply outlets. The projection developed by Mercator soon became the standard representation of the earth and remains so today. The original map was large and complex, but one can get a good idea of its contents by using this simplified outline from G. R. Crone's *Maps and Their Makers* (5th edition, 1978), p. 77.

WORKING WITH SPACE

1. The essence of Mercator's projection is that all the meridians cross the parallels at right angles. The distance between each parallel is then increased as the map moves poleward in a ratio to accommodate the curvature of the earth. The effect of all this is to make any straight line on the map also a straight line on the surface of the earth. This was a great help to navigation. Draw a straight line on the map from the mouth of the Amazon River to the English Channel. A navigator can measure the angle at which this line crosses a parallel and set a course on a compass following this angle to reach port.

2. Note that Mercator provided a detailed explanation of the projection in a box covering the unknown parts of North America. A companion box in the south Pacific explained how accurate distances could be calculated from the data provided on the map. Since the map was scientifically constructed, it could be used as a reference tool as well as an illustration. A diagram for navigators on how to figure courses was provided at the lower right. Use a marking pen to highlight these boxes containing technical explanations.

3. Other boxes scattered throughout the map provided notes on how Mercator obtained the geographic information that appeared on his map. He was not always correct. The note on the Ganges, for example, reveals that he confused it with the River of Canton in Marco Polo. The inset map of the North Polar Region at the lower left was needed because the nature of the projection made it almost impossible to show the polar regions. Mercator used an old tradition to show the region about the North Pole, which revealed a definite Northwest Passage around North America.

PLACES

What name did Mercator use for:

_____ 1. the Americas

_____ 2. Mexico

_____ 3. the Indian Ocean

_____ 4. the Arctic Ocean

_____ 5. the Bering Strait

_____ 6. Antarctica

EXTENSIONS

Write a brief commentary on another one of Mercator's maps (for example, one pictures the world in two heart–shapes) or on any map by his contemporary, Abraham Ortelius.

HarperCollins Publishers © 1991

Wall of the Farmers General

Seine River

La Bastille

The Temple

TEMPLE

RUE ST ANTOINE

Hôtel de Ville

Île St. Louis

RUE DU TEMPLE

RUE ST MARTIN

RUE ST DENIS

Notre Dame Cathedral

Île de La Cité

Ste. Geneviève (Pantheon)

RUE MONTMARTRE

Sorbonne

Pont au Change

ST HONORÉ

Palais Royal

Pont Neuf

RUE DE LA HARPE

Louvre

RUE ST JACQUES

BLVD DESITALIENS

RUE DE RICHELIEU

RUE

Tuileries Palace

Palaces

D'ENFER

Place Vendôme

St. Germain des Prés

Luxembourg Palace

RUE

Tuileries Gardens

St. Sulpice

SEVRES

DE VAURIGARD

Place de Louis XV

Pont de la Concorde

Pont Royal

RUE DE

RUE DE

Champs Elisées

Hôtel des Invalides

Champ de Mars

Ecole Militaire

Wall of the Farmers General

Seine River

HarperCollins Publishers © 1991

TOPIC 22
Paris in 1789 A.D.

BACKGROUND

The first reason for a city, Lewis Mumford noted in his monumental study of *The City in History* (1961), was as a ceremonial meeting place. In its origins many a city began as a magnet, a place that pulled people together in quest of a better life. Open to outsiders, the early city grew because it was a goal for pilgrims. Later it became a container, storing behind walls a variety of goods, people, institutions, and traditions. Over time a map of the city often became a record of its history.

PLACES

Paris in 1789 had already celebrated 1800 birthdays since the Romans planted an outpost among a group of Celts who made a living by fishing. The first site and still the center of Paris in 1789 was the island of the city. Here **(1)** _____ is located, dating from the 1300s. The city soon spread to both banks of the **(2)** _____ River, and important buildings clustered about the site. The **(3)** _____ , today a celebrated art museum, began as a fort about 1200 but was later remodeled and expanded to serve as a royal palace. The **(4)** _____ , originally a school of theology founded about 1200, remained in place in 1789 but later took on a new role as part of the University of Paris and moved to a new site.

Medieval walls could be traced in the street patterns and in remnants of fortifications adapted to other purposes such as the **(5)** _____ , a fortress built about 1370 but used in 1789 as a prison. The city hall, or **(6)** _____ , occupied a prominent site opposite the cathedral. On the other side of the river stood the new church of **(7)** _____ , named in honor of the city's patron saint whose prayers spared Paris from an attack by Attila the Hun in 451 The Division of Christianity, c. 1550 A.D. In 1791 the church would be renamed the **(8)** _____ and be converted into a monument for national heroes.

The **(9)** _____ Palace near the church dated from the early 17th century. The **(10)** _____ , located west of the celebrated Tuileries Gardens, dates from 1718 and today is the official residence of the president of France.

Louis XV built the Hotel **(11)** _____ in the 1670s to house needy veterans of his wars. The military school and the parade ground, **(12)** _____ , were located nearby. The Eiffel Tower now occupies the site where cadets paraded in 1789. The Wall of the Farmers General was erected in the 1780s to facilitate the collection of import taxes. It was not a major fortification.

EXTENSIONS

Find another map of Paris and write a brief commentary comparing it with this map. In what ways is the new map a reminder of various aspects of the city's history? Does it confirm Mumford's observation about the city being a magnet and a container?

1500 A.D.

1525

1550

1575

1600

1625

1650

1675

1700

1725

1750 A.D.

HarperCollins Publishers © 1991

TOPIC 23
Early Modern Times: A Chronological Context

BACKGROUND

History tells a continuous story, and the division of its tale into periods can be a dangerous practice unless we realize that these are merely devices invented to help our understanding. The years 1500 and 1750, used as the end dates for this timeline, were selected as much for their rounded-ness and the size of the page as their historical significance. Perhaps 1492 would be a better starting date, and the period maybe should be extended up to 1789, 1815, or 1848. Nevertheless, this chart will be helpful in assisting you to integrate major developments in politics, religion, art, music, and science.

WORKING WITH TIME

1. The division of this timeline into five-year intervals makes it convenient to chart the lifetimes of individual people. Use the column on the right to chart the following celebrated figures of the period. Draw a line parallel to the main stem and a short space to the right to represent each person's lifespan. Some lines will overlap, so be sure to separate them. Label each one.

    a. Luther, 1483–1546

    b. Elizabeth I, 1533–1603

    c. Galileo, 1564–1642

    d. Louis XIV, 1638–1715

    e. Newton, 1642–1727

    f. Bach, 1685–1750

2. Record the following events in the left column of the chart in the appropriate places:

1517	Luther's *95 Theses*
1519	Magellan's crew: circumnavigation of the globe
1536	Calvin's *Institutes*
1545	Council of Trent
1556	Philip II becomes king of Spain
1588	Defeat of Spanish Armada
1598	Edict of Nantes
1618–48	Thirty Years' War
1649–60	Puritan Rule in England
1688	Glorious Revolution England
1696	Peter the Great becomes czar
1701–14	War of the Spanish Succession
1712	Invention of the steam engine
1730	Methodist movement begins
1733	Flying shuttle patented in England
c. 1750	Rise of Neoclassical movement

EXTENSIONS

Write a brief biography of one of the people listed on right-hand column. Try to incorporate some of the events listed in the left-hand column in your sketch.

HarperCollins Publishers © 1991

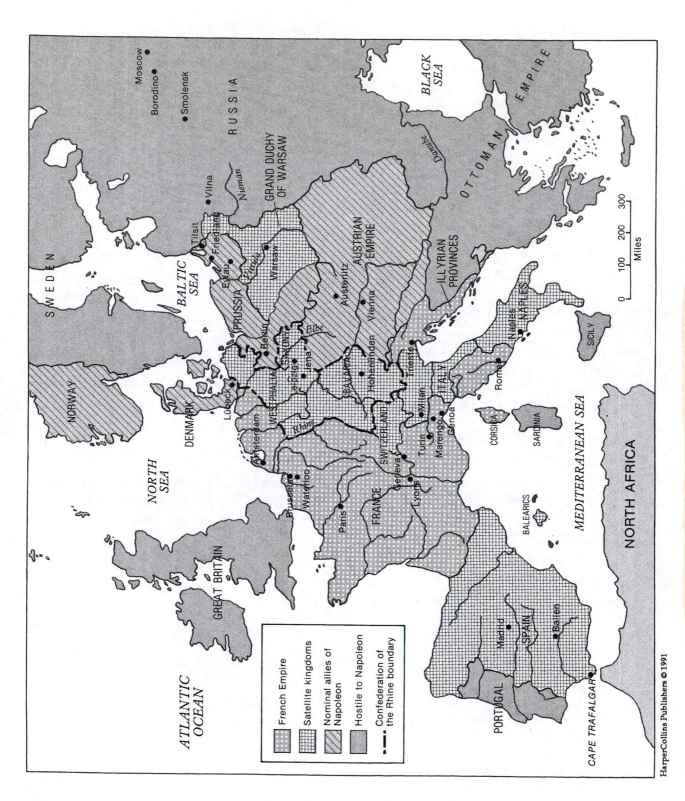

HarperCollins Publishers © 1991

TOPIC 24
Europe in 1810 A.D.

BACKGROUND

In 1810 Napoleon was at the zenith of his power. During that year he married Marie Louise of Austria, confiscated British goods on the continent, and annexed important seaports in Germany. Meanwhile, the spirit of independence was marching through Latin America and Simon Bolivar had emerged as the leading figure in fashioning a new order in the old Spanish Empire. Just two years earlier Beethoven had completed his fifth symphony and Goethe had published the first part of "Faust." The ominous opening statements in each work signaled that this map of Europe would not last another five years.

PLACES

1. In 1796 Napoleon led a French army to northern Italy. A series of victories over Austria and Sardinia led to a treaty in which France received control of the Austrian Netherlands. This was an important commercial region extending from the English Channel to the Rhine River. It included the cities of Brussels and Cologne. Shade this region on the map, label it, and date it 1796.

2. After Napoleon's heroic return to Paris, the Directory, anxious to get him out of the country, sent him on an expedition against the Turkish Empire in Egypt. After initial successes, Napeoleon's troops were cut off by the British fleet that came to aid the Turks. Meanwhile French troops in Italy had suffered defeat and the government of the Directory was tottering in Paris. Napoleon slipped out of Egypt, crossing the Mediterranean in a small boat. Returning to Paris in 1799, he took over the government and became First Consul. Indicate Napoleon's route to Egypt and his return on the map. Label it "To Egypt and Back, 1798–99."

3. In 1800 Napoleon led a French Army across the Alps into the Po Valley. Once again he defeated the Austrians at Marengo. This led to the formal end of the Holy Roman Empire. A few years later Napoleon annexed the region from Turin to Genoa to France and became president of the Italian Republic. Circle Marengo and date it 1800.

4. Following a peace with Britain, Napoleon was crowned emperor in 1804. War followed the next year and Napoleon defeated the Austrian and Russian armies at Austerlitz, northeast of Vienna. Circle Austerlitz and date it.

5. Napoleon then set out to remake the map of Europe. He made one of his brothers king of Naples and set up the Confederation of the Rhine under French protection. This led to war with Prussia and another French victory at Jena in 1806. Shade the Kingdom of Naples and the Confederation of the Rhine. Circle Jena. Date these places 1806.

6. Further battles with Russia ended when Czar Alexander I met Napoleon near Tilsit in 1807 and recognized French control of the Grand Duchy of Warsaw. Circle Tilsit, color the Grand Duchy of Warsaw, and date them.

7. In 1808 a French army invaded Spain. Napoleon appointed his brother Joseph king of Spain, but British troops arrived to oppose this move. The Peninsular War in Spain was still going on in 1810, the date of this map. Color Spain and date it 1808.

8. War broke out again between France and Austria in 1809. It lasted only four months, ending when a French army entered Vienna. Napoleon then divorced Josephine and prepared to marry the daughter of the Austrian Emperor. Also in 1809 France annexed the Papal States in Italy. Circle Vienna and color the Papal States. Date both places 1809.

EXTENSIONS

While Napoleon was remaking the map of Europe between 1796 and 1810, changes were also taking place in the Americas. Write a brief paper on how events in the Americas during this period were connected to the Napoleonic Wars in Europe.

HarperCollins Publishers © 1991

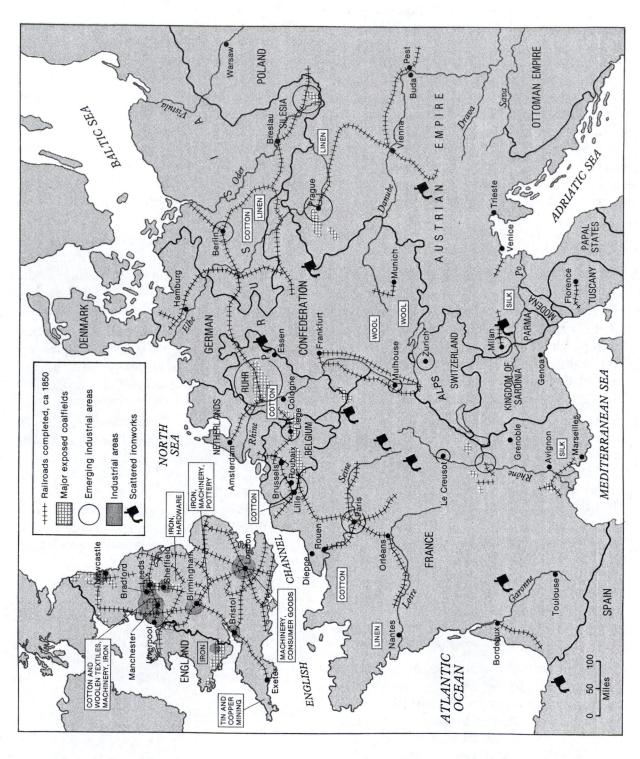

TOPIC 25
European Industrialization, c. 1850 A.D.

BACKGROUND

The year 1850 was quite a time for European culture. Elizabeth Barrett Browning wrote the "Sonnets from the Portuguese." Alfred, Lord Tennyson, became poet laureate in England. Herbert Spencer published *Social Statics,* marking the beginnings of sociology. Richard Wagner composed "Lohengrin" with its famous wedding march. Jean Francois Millet painted "The Sower." Joseph Paxton built the Crystal Palace for the first great world's fair. And Robert Stephenson's cast-iron railroad bridge was put into service in Newcastle, England.

Traditional values remained, but a new era had arrived. It was an age of steam and machines; of iron, steel, and glass; of science and technology; of invention and progress. The Crystal Palace reached a height of 108 feet and covered 19 acres. It held over 10,000 exhibits divided into four categories: raw materials, machinery, manufactured goods, and the arts. The purpose of the exposition was to demonstrate the progress made in each field and, by the way, to celebrate England's leadership in the Industrial Revolution.

PLACES

1. Use a pen to highlight the railroads on the map. Then mark the following statements as true or false in 1850.

    _____ a. England had the most extensive system of railroads in Europe.

    _____ b. One could go by train from Paris to Marseilles.

    _____ c. Munich was a hub for many railroad lines.

    _____ d. Railroads were very popular in the Po Valley.

    _____ e. Paris and London were both railroad centers.

2. Coal became a key raw material in the age of steam power. Color the major coal regions brown. They are listed below:

    a. Newcastle
    b. southern Wales
    c. Ruhr valley
    d. southern Belgium
    e. Luxembourg
    f. Bohemia
    g. near Lyon

3. Use a marking pen to highlight the major existing and emerging industrial areas in Europe in 1850. Identify the following industrial areas:

    _____ a. on the Irish Sea

    _____ b. in Switzerland

    _____ c. on the Seine River

    _____ d. in Prussia

    _____ e. near Cologne, along a tributary of the Rhine River

4. In 1850 small ironworks were scattered across Europe. Two of these were located near:

    _____ a. the Po Valley

    _____ b. Prussia (Westphalia)

5. Match the following cities or regions with their major manufactured goods or raw materials in 1850:

    _____ a. Sheffield

    _____ b. Lille

    _____ c. Nantes

    _____ d. Cornwall

    _____ e. Marseilles

EXTENSIONS

Find a map of one of the following early industrial centers showing the layout of a 19th-century industrial city: Leeds, Liverpool, Birmingham, Manchester, or Sheffield. Write a commentary on the map.

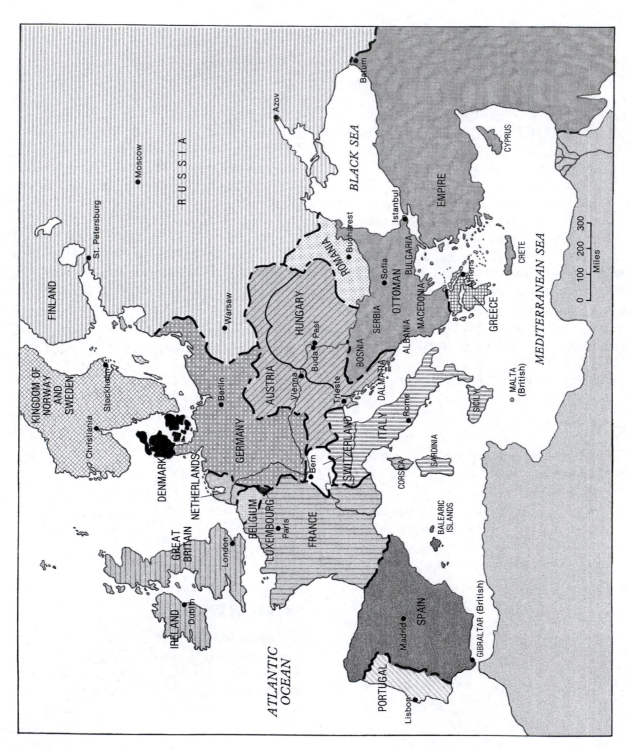

ATLANTIC OCEAN

IRELAND
Dublin

GREAT BRITAIN
London

KINGDOM OF NORWAY AND SWEDEN
Stockholm
Christiania

FINLAND

St. Petersburg

Moscow

R U S S I A

Warsaw

DENMARK

NETHERLANDS

BELGIUM

LUXEMBOURG

Paris

FRANCE

GERMANY
Berlin

SWITZERLAND
Bern

AUSTRIA
Vienna

HUNGARY
Buda Pest

Trieste

ITALY
Rome

CORSICA

SARDINIA

BALEARIC ISLANDS

PORTUGAL
Lisbon

SPAIN
Madrid

GIBRALTAR (British)

DALMATIA

BOSNIA

SERBIA

ROMANIA
Bucharest

BLACK SEA

Azov

Batum

OTTOMAN EMPIRE

BULGARIA
Sofia

MACEDONIA

ALBANIA

Istanbul

GREECE
Athens

MALTA (British)

SICILY

CRETE

CYPRUS

MEDITERRANEAN SEA

0 100 200 300
Miles

HarperCollins Publishers © 1991

TOPIC 26
Europe in 1871

BACKGROUND

In 1871 Prussia defeated France in the Franco–Prussian War and Italy was united with its capital at Rome. In England, Charles Darwin published *The Descent of Man* and in Cairo, Giuseppe Verdi's opera, "Aida," was performed for the first time. The pace of change continued to keep the mapmakers busy. Hardly a year had gone by in the last seven decades without some border change in Europe. The map of Europe in 1871 therefore looks unstable to those who look at it through the spectacles of history. Nevertheless, 1871 was a good year to take stock of the political geography of the continent.

PLACES

1. Locate the Baltic Sea. Note that in 1871 four nations controlled all the land along its shores. _____ controlled the straits leading to the _____ Sea. _____ controlled the entire southern shoreline. The _____ Empire included Finland. The Kingdom of _____ and _____ occupied the Scandinavian Peninsula. Label the Baltic Sea.

2. On the Balkan Peninsula, most of the territory was controlled by the _____ Empire. _____ , along the Adriatic coast, was a province of Hungrary. Label the Adriatic Sea.

3. In the Mediterranean Sea, the islands of Crete and Cyprus remained part of the _____ Empire. Sicily and Sardinia were incorporated in the new kingdom of _____ . Corsica, the birthplace of Napoleon, was a province of _____ .

Two strategic places in the Mediterranean were British colonial possessions: _____ and _____. A British fleet was a major factor in the region in 1871. The Suez Canal, constructed by a company owned by France and Britain, opened in 1869. Label the Suez Canal.

4. France lost Alsace–Lorraine to the German Empire in 1871 as a result of the _____ War. These regions, located west of the Rhine River, were regained by France after World War I. Color them on the map. During the course of the war, the third French republic was proclaimed and the Commune briefly ruled Paris. Circle Paris and label the French republic on the map.

5. In 1871 Karl Marx continued writing in _____ where he was nearing the end of his life as an exile. Nikolai Lenin, who would become his most famous disciple, was just a year old, learning to walk. His name was Vladimir Ilyich Ulyanov until he adopted "Lenin" later in life. Lenin was born in a town on the Volga River about 400 miles east of Moscow. On your map indicate these milestones in the appropriate location: Marx, d. 1883; Lenin, b. 1870.

EXTENSIONS

Develop an outline for a magazine article that would have appeared in January, 1872. The purpose of the article is to review the events of 1871. Use this map as the featured illustration for the review.

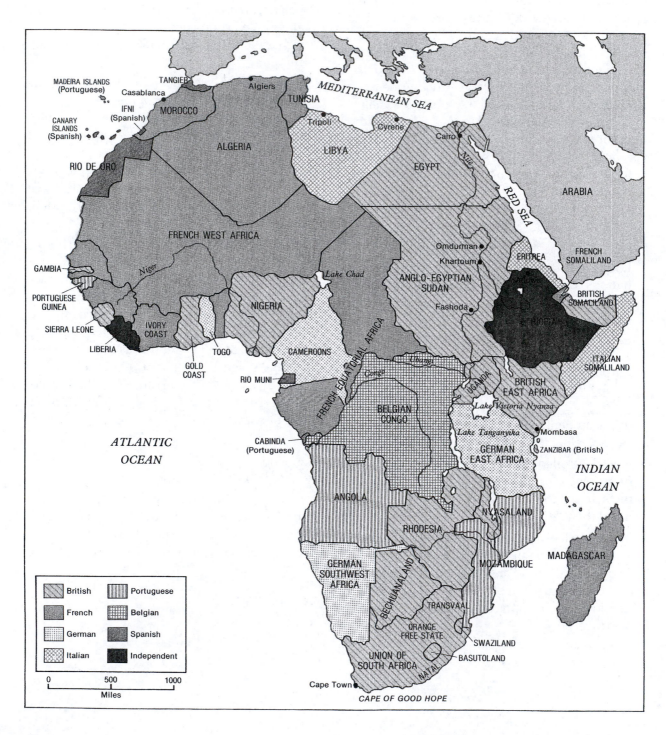

TOPIC 27
Africa on the Eve of World War I

BACKGROUND

North Africa as a part of the Mediterranean basin had been associated with Western civilization from the earliest period. The expansion of Islam, however, divided the sea into two distinct culture regions. In the 19th century European powers expanded their interest in African territories. The whole continent, with only two exceptions, was soon divided between various European nations.

PLACES

1. Use a marking pen to highlight the four major river systems of Africa: Nile, Niger, Congo (and the Ubangi), and Zambezi (label it on the map).

2. Note the great lakes in East Africa. Lakes Victoria and Tanganyika both drain into the _____ river system. Lake Nyasa sends its waters to the _____ River.

3. Label Africa's two great deserts: the Sahara and the Kalahari. The Tropic of _____ crosses the former and the Tropic of _____ crosses the latter.

4. Draw the equator on the map. In the west it crosses the _____ basin; in east Africa it crosses Lake _____.

WORKING WITH SPACE AND TIME

1. The Spanish and Portuguese established the earliest colonies in Africa. Spain claimed the Canary Islands in 1497 and Portugal established colonies on the Indian (Mozambique) and the Atlantic (Angola) coasts in 1505 and 1576 respectively. Date these regions.

2. French interests on Madagascar date from about 1642. Place this date on the map.

3. The British developed a trading plantation in Sierra Leone about 1737 and the Spanish added the island of Fernando Po (off the Cameroons) about 1787. Add these dates to your map.

4. The British established colonies at Cape Town (1814), Gambia (1816), and Natal (1842). Spain added outposts along the Atlantic coast at Guinea (Rio Muni) and Ifni in 1842 and 1860. France claimed Somaliland and Algiers in 1802 and 1830. Add these dates to the map.

5. Use a marking pen to highlight areas of Africa under European influence at the middle of the 19th century.

6. Industrialization led to a search of raw materials and markets in overseas areas. Improvements in transportation, especially railroads and steamboats, opened up possibilities for settlements and colonies in the interior. After 1870 the race for colonies began in earnest. Draw a possible route for a Cairo to Capetown railroad which Cecil Rhodes advocated as a way to extend British imperial interests across the continent.

7. Record the dates for British control of the following areas on your map: Egypt, 1882; Anglo–Egyptian Sudan, 1889; British East Africa, 1895; Nyasaland, 1891; Rhodesia, 1889; and Bechuanaland, 1885.

8. French colonies took an east-west orientation. Date the following: Tunisia, 1881; Ivory Coast, 1893; French Equatorial Africa, 1885–95; French West Africa, 1911; Morocco, 1911.

9. Although Belgian interests in the Congo dated from the 1880s, the Belgian Congo did not become an official colony until 1908. Meanwhile, the Germans had acquired Togoland and South West Africa in 1884 and German East Africa in 1890. Date these areas.

10. Italy was a latecomer to African colonization, taking Italian Somaliland in 1889, Eritrea in 1890, and Libya in 1912. Date these regions.

EXTENSIONS

Develop a color code and use it to show the areas claimed by the various European nations in 1914. Add a legend to the map discussing the reasons for imperialism in Africa.

HarperCollins Publishers © 1991

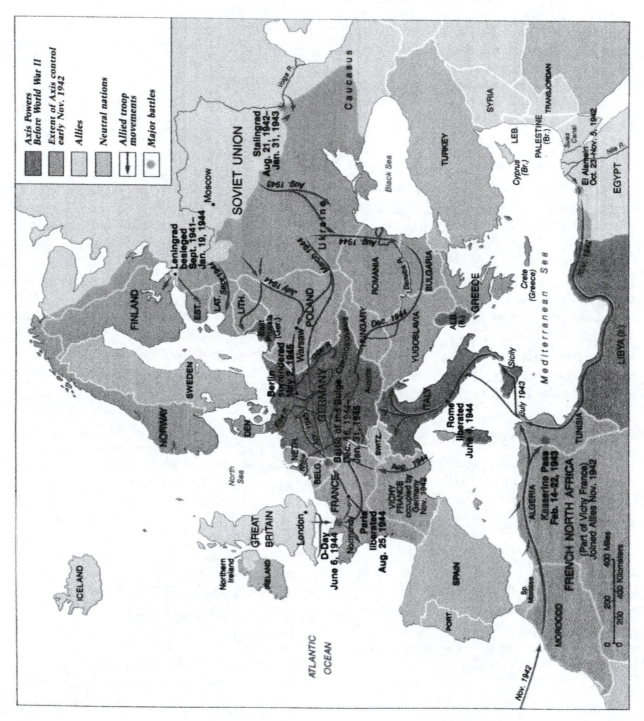

HarperCollins Publishers © 1991

TOPIC 28
World War II in Europe and North Africa

BACKGROUND

In August 1939, Germany and Russia signed a non-aggression pact that cleared the way for the Nazi invasion of Poland on September 1. The Russian armies then entered Poland from the east and by the end of the month an independent Poland had once again been swallowed up by its neighbors. Less than two years later the tables were turned, and Hitler began Operation Barbarossa, the Nazi invasion of Russia. In the fall of 1941 German forces met their first serious reverses. They failed to take Leningrad and were defeated in a massed tank and artillery battle at El Alamein in Egypt. German expansion had reached its greatest extent.

PLACES

1. This is a complex map. The best place to start an exposition of it is by noting the date of its base. November 1942 was the high tide of Axis expansion in Europe and North Africa. Draw a bold line indicating the territory controlled by the Axis powers at this time.

2. Shade the nations that were neutral in World War II: Sweden, Ireland, Switzerland, Turkey, Portugal, and Spain.

3. The lines and arrows trace Allied troop movements as they liberated the conquered territory and invaded the Axis nations. Reference dates for key battles help fit the action together into proper chronological sequence. Place the following events in order, indicating **A** for the earliest, **B** for the next, and so on. Then place each letter on the map in its proper location:

_____ Normandy invasion

_____ Kasserine Pass

_____ Stalingrad siege begins

_____ Liberation of Rome

_____ Surrender of Berlin

_____ Battle of the Bulge

4. France was occupied by Germany in November 1942, when an accommodation with the enemy was reached by the Vichy government. At the same time France's North African colonies officially joined the Allies and an Allied force landed in _____ on the Atlantic Ocean.

5. D–Day, the code name for the _____ invasion, was_____, 1944. It was scheduled to occur after the Axis Forces had been pushed back in the "soft underbelly" of Europe. Rome was liberated on _____, _____ days before D–Day.

EXTENSIONS

Using this map, describe the action in the European theater of World War II between November 1942 and 1945. Before this date the Axis powers won a long series of battles. Then the tide turned. You could describe each year's events in a separate paragraph.

HarperCollins Publishers © 1991

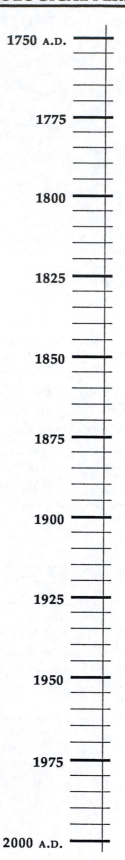

1750 A.D.

1775

1800

1825

1850

1875

1900

1925

1950

1975

2000 A.D.

HarperCollins Publishers © 1991

TOPIC 29
Modern Europe: A Chronological Perspective

BACKGROUND

The history of the United States is part and parcel of the story of modern Europe. One part of the tale cannot be fully told without reference to events across the Atlantic Ocean. The Declaration of Independence can also be seen as a turning point in history, heralding the emergence of a modern Europe when the principles of Enlightenment thought were put into practice. Thus a chronological perspective on modern Europe can be effectively developed for American students by placing the major events in American history and Western civilization side by side.

WORKING WITH TIME

1. Start with American history and label it on the left-hand side of the chart. Enter about 25 key dates but be sure to include the following:

1756–63	Great War for Empire
1776	Declaration of Independence
1787	Constitutional Convention
1803	Louisiana Purchase
1823	Monroe Doctrine
1846	War with Mexico
1861–65	Civil War
1869	Transcontinental railroad
1898	Spanish–American War
1918	Fourteen Points
1929	Great Depression begins
1941	Pearl Harbor
1947	Marshall Plan
1962	Cuban Missile Crisis
1973	End of Vietnam War
1980s	"Computer revolution"
1990	Kuwait crisis

2. Now use the right-hand side of the chart to record the following dates in the history of Western civilization.

c. 1760	Enlightenment at its height
1776	*Wealth of Nations* by Adam Smith
1789	French Revolution
1804	Napoleon becomes emperor
1815	Congress of Vienna
1830	Revolutionary movements
1845	Irish famine
1848	Revolutionary movements, *Communist Manifesto*
1859	*Origin of Species* by Charles Darwin
1869	Suez Canal
1870	Franco–Prussian War
1879	Dual Alliance
1898	German naval program
1904	Entente between Britain and France
1914–19	World War I
1917	Russian Revolution
1922	Mussolini in power
1933	Hitler in power
1938	Munich Conference
1939–45	World War II
1949	Formation of NATO
1955	Warsaw Pact
1957	European Economic Community
1962	Second Vatican Council
1975	Helsinki Conference
1980	Solidarity Movement
1986	Chernobyl disaster
1989	Berlin wall removed

EXTENSIONS

1. Select a nation in Europe and write a brief account of its modern history relating it to the events listed on *both* sides of this chart.

2. Or, write a brief account of the relationships between the history of the United States and the development of modern Europe. Use this chart as a basic reference.

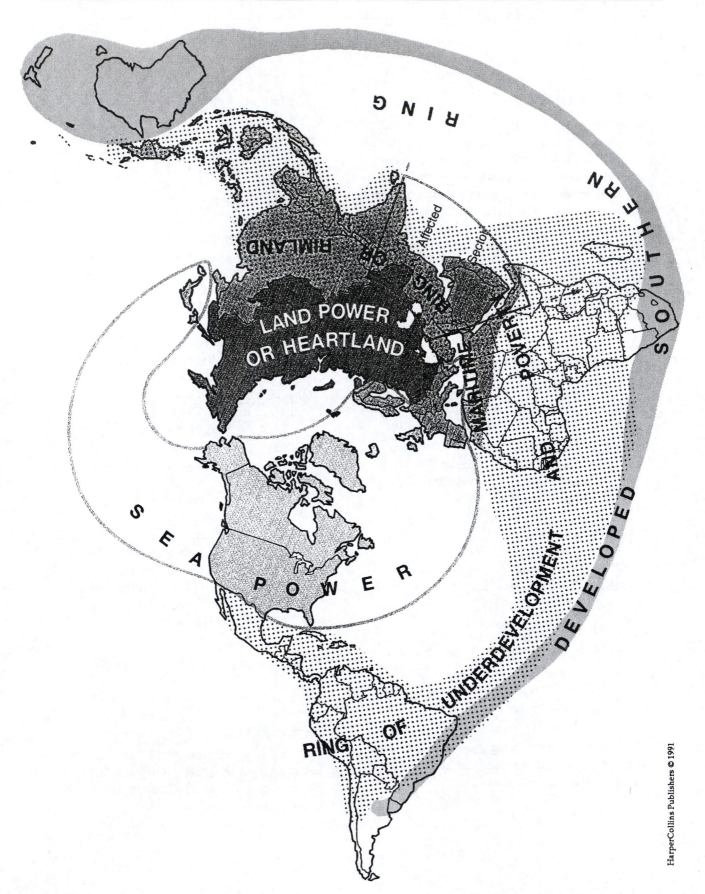

LAND POWER OR HEARTLAND

RIMLAND

RING

SEA POWER

RING OF UNDERDEVELOPMENT AND DEVELOPED SOUTHERN

MARITIME POWER

Affected Section

TOPIC 30
The World in 1975

BACKGROUND

This map reflects the ideas of Sir Halford MacKinder (1861–1947), a British political geographer. His essay on "The Geographical Pivot of History" suggested that the pivot of modern history would be a line between Moscow and Novosibitsk, the city where the Trans-Siberian Railroad crossed the Ob River.

This was a breathtaking hypothesis in 1904. Russia was then a backward agrarian nation,e suffering defeat in the Russo–Japanese War. In 1947, when Mackinder died, his ideas had been fully vindicated.

Actually Mackinder modified his thesis as time went on, selecting the suggestive name "Heartland" for the original idea of a pivot area. He was struck by the difference between imperial expansion over land and over sea routes. The land-based state was a natural fortress and, if it had access to the right combination of resources, it could make a bid for world dominance.

Eventually Mackinder's theory was reduced to three simple axioms: (1) The nation that controlled Eastern Europe would command the Heartland. (2) The Heartland was in a position to dominate the World Island, or the Afro–Eurasian land mass. (3) Domination of the World Island would lead to supremacy throughout the globe.

PLACES

Label the following cities on the map and indicate the realm or ring to which they belong:

1. Moscow _____
2. Washington _____
3. Buenos Aires _____
4. Tokyo _____
5. Calcutta _____
6. London _____
7. Mexico City _____
8. Paris _____
9. Lagos _____
10. Cairo _____

WORKING WITH SPACE

1. The Heartland or "Land Power" on this map includes all of the Soviet Union plus some adjacent territories. The boundary of this region in Europe was called the _____ by Winston Churchill.

2. The "Sea Power" was often called the "Free World" in the West. It was centered on the Midland Ocean and was best represented by the _____ _____ Organization.

3. Note the extension of the Sea Power region across the Pacific Ocean to include _____. This adjusted Mackinder's original concept.

4. The Maritime Ring or _____ had the potential to rival the Sea Power group and the Heartland, but it was fragmented into four mculture regions and dozens of nations.

5. The "Ring of _____ and _____" was also called the Southern Realm. Note how this ring overlaps the _____ .

6. The "Developed Southern Ring" collected outlying regions that were offspring of the Sea Power group. Developed industrial economies could be found in the southern reaches of _____ .

EXTENSIONS

Use this map to illustrate a feature article about what the world looked like on January 1, 1975. Select any city in the places section as the location for this newspaper. Note that 1975 was the year of Conference on Security and Cooperation that met in Helsinki, Finland.

HarperCollins Publishers © 1991

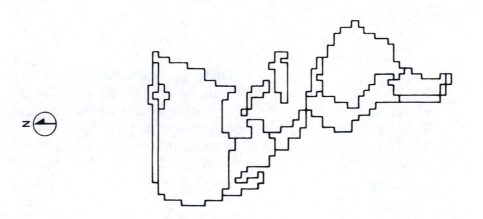

Z

HarperCollins Publishers © 1991

TOPIC 31
World Population Cartogram, 1975

BACKGROUND

A cartogram is a graph that looks like a map. As in a pie graph, the area allotted to each category is proportional to the data presented in the topic, in this case the population of each major nation in 1975. The shape and location of each segment of the graph is drawn by an artist to suggest the position of the nation on a world map. Thus Canada, at the upper left-hand side of the cartogram, is pictured as a thin sliver of a nation although in real extent it is the world's second largest nation. Its population, however, was only about 40 percent of that of Mexico. Mexico thus is portrayed as much larger in size.

The cartogram originally appeared in Jean Mayer, "The Dimensions of Human Hunger," *Scientific American* (1976).

PLACES

Label the following nations on the cartogram. Each of these is considered a large nation and had a population in excess of 20 million in 1875.

1. North America

   a. Canada   **b.** United States   **c.** Mexico

   (Note that Cuba, the rest of the West Indies, and Central America are represented as units.)

2. South America

   a. Brazil   **b.** Argentina

   (Note that the other nations of South America are grouped together in units such as the Andean and Caribbean regions.)

3. Europe

   a. United Kingdom   **e.** West Germany
      (Britain)
   b. France   **f.** Poland
   c. Spain   **g.** Rumania
   d. Italy   **h.** Soviet Union

   (Note that these were the only European nations with a population of more than 20 million in 1975.)

4. Africa

   a. Egypt   **d.** Ethiopia
   b. Morocco   **e.** Zaire
   c. Nigeria   **f.** South Africa

5. Middle East

   a. Turkey   **b.** Iran

6. Asia (continental)

   a. China   **e.** Burma
   b. India   **f.** South Korea
   c. Pakistan   **g.** Thailand
   d. Bangladesh   **h.** Vietnam

7. Pacific Rim

   a. Japan   **b.** Philippines   **c.** Indonesia

8. There were seven nations with populations exceeding 100 million in 1975. The two largest, _____ and _____, were both on the Asian mainland. The third and fourth largest were considered to be the world's superpowers: _____ in Europe and Asia and _____ in North America. Further down on the list were _____ on the islands of southeast Asia, _____ in South America, and _____ on the islands of East Asia.

EXTENSIONS

Locate an article on the world's population in the last quarter of the 20th century. Write a summary of the article listing its major points, and add a conclusion that relates the article to some major themes in Western civilization.

Ethnic Composition.

According to preliminary data from the 1989 Soviet census, Russians comprise 50.8% of the total population of the Soviet Union. In the chart below, each rectangle represents roughly one-half of one percent (.005) of the total population of the USSR, about 1.43 million people. The 22 nationalities represented here comprise almost 95% of the total Soviet population. All figures are rounded off.

CH Chuvash	ML Moldavian	AR Armenian	BA Bashkir
E Estonian	MR Mordvin	AZ Azerbaijani	BE Belorussian
G Georgian	P Polish		
D German	R Russian		
J Jewish	TJ Tajik		
KZ Kazakh	TA Tatar		
KI Kirghiz	TU Turkmen		
LA Latvian	UK Ukrainian		
LI Lithuanian	UZ Uzbek		

HarperCollins Publishers © 1991

The Soviet Union: Ethnic Composition in 1989

BACKGROUND

This is another type of cartogram developed by Leo Dillon in the Office of the Geographer of the U.S. Department of State. He used data from the 1989 Soviet census to "map out" the ethnic composition of the U.S.S.R. Each rectangle represents one half of one percent of the total population. The units are then coded by ethnic type and arranged so that they suggest the geographic location of the ethic groups. About five percent of the population is made up of very small groups that are represented by blank spaces on the graph.

WORKING WITH SPACE

1. Each block in the cartogram represents about 1.5 million people. Thus the Baltic ethnic groups get four squares. The _____ people in the northwest corner get one rectangle, while their neighbors, the _____ and _____ , get one and two respectively.

2. Judging by this cartogram one could guess that most of the 1.5 million Polish people in the Soviet Union lived in the _____ Republic.

3. Since the Russian people made up about 51 percent of the population, _____ of the 200 squares are marked with an R.

4. The second largest ethnic group in the U.S.S.R. is _____.

5. The Moldavian people had their own republic in the far _____ corner of the U.S.S.R.

6. The Georgian, Azerbaijani, and Armenian peoples occupy the region between the _____ and the _____ seas, accounting for about _____ percent of the total Soviet population.

7. In Central Asia the _____ people are the largest ethnic group, accounting for six percent of the total Soviet population.

8. The Kazakh people who live in the steppes north and west of the Caspian Sea make up _____ percent of the U.S.S.R. population.

9. The _____ , _____ , and _____ peoples occupy soviet republics in central Asia along the U.S.S.R.'s southern border between the Caspian Sea and the Tien Shan mountains.

10. Jews and Germans are two minority groups in the Soviet Union, each of which numbers between _____ and _____ million people according to the 1989 Soviet census.

EXTENSIONS

Select an ethnic group represented on this map and develop a timeline to show its history from the earliest times up to the present. You may adapt one of the extra timelines in the appendix.

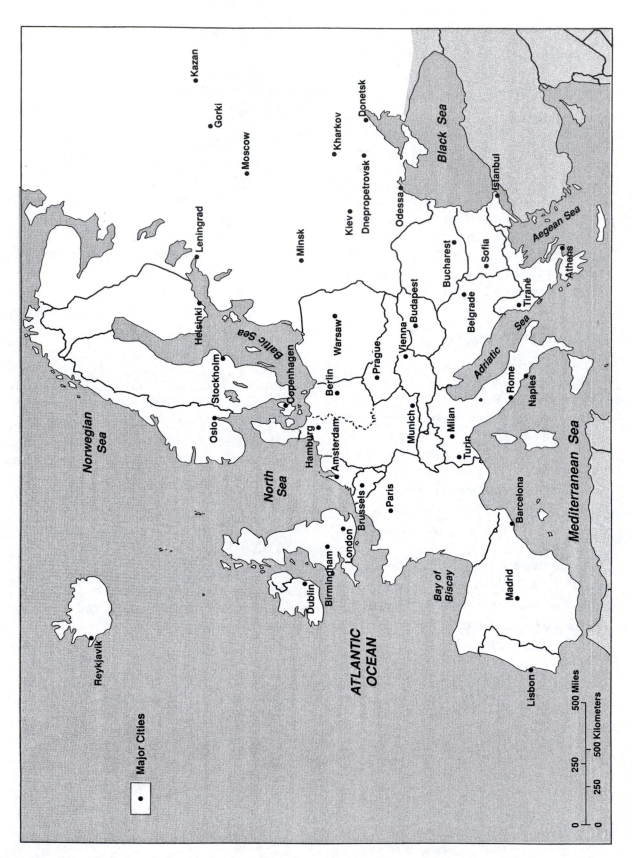

Major Cities

• Major Cities

Norwegian Sea

North Sea

Baltic Sea

ATLANTIC OCEAN

Bay of Biscay

Mediterranean Sea

Adriatic Sea

Aegean Sea

Black Sea

• Kazan

• Gorki

• Moscow

• Leningrad

• Helsinki

• Minsk

• Kharkov

• Dnepropetrovsk

• Kiev

• Odessa

• Istanbul

• Bucharest

• Sofia

• Athens

• Tiranë

• Belgrade

• Budapest

• Vienna

• Warsaw

• Berlin

• Prague

• Stockholm

• Copenhagen

• Oslo

• Hamburg

• Amsterdam

• Munich

• Milan

• Turin

• Rome

• Naples

• Barcelona

• Brussels

• Paris

• London

• Birmingham

• Dublin

• Reykjavik

• Madrid

• Lisbon

500 Miles

500 Kilometers

250

250

0

0

HarperCollins Publishers © 1991

TOPIC 33
Europe: Major Cities, 1990

BACKGROUND

European cities have been extolled as testaments to the glories of civilization. Thus it is helpful to review a map of Europe's major cities near the end of a course in the history of Western civilization.

WORKING WITH SPACE

1. Most of the cities on this map can be placed into one of two categories: river towns and seaports. Some will fit into both categories. London, for example, is located at the first convenient bridging spot on the Thames River, but it is also a major seaport. Circle London on the map. Then connect it by sea routes to the following cities: Leningrad, Istanbul, Barcelona, and Amsterdam

2. Vienna, located on the Danube River, is a focal point for inland transportation routes. As the center of the Austrian–Hungarian Empire, it constantly looked south to the Adriatic for an outlet to the sea. Circle Vienna and the following cities that also lie in the Danube basin: Munich, Belgrade, Budapest, and Bucharest. Draw arrows from Vienna and Munich toward the Adriatic Sea.

3. Madrid is an exceptional city. Box it. It is certainly not a seaport and, although it is located on a tributary of the Tagus River, it is not much of a river city. Overland transportation routes radiate from Madrid in every direction except down the Tagus valley. Indicate the general direction of these routes on your map.

4. Moscow is located near the headwaters of both the Volga and the Don rivers. Located on the North European Plain, it has convenient access to the Caspian and the Black seas. Circle Moscow on the map and draw arrows to indicate the direction of these natural gateways. Then draw a dotted line to connect Moscow with Leningrad, which was built by Peter the Great to give Russia a window to the West.

5. Berlin and Warsaw are major cities on the North European Plain. Both are connected by rivers and canals with extensive regions draining into the Baltic Sea. Hamburg, located at the head of a large estuary, is both a seaport and a river city. The Elbe River reaches from Hanburg to Prague and is also connected by canals with Berlin. Draw a box around these cities.

6. Paris is a river city that is situated so that it not only commands the Seine River basin but also has convenient transportation links to nearly every part of France. It is the hub of the French wheel. Draw this "wheel" on the map.

7. Amsterdam, Brussels, and other cities in the Low Countries serve a rich hinterland that reaches back to Switzerland along the Rhine Valley. Enclose this region with a line.

PLACES

Which city is:

_____	1. Spain's major Mediterranean port
_____	2. The Ukraine's major port
_____	3. The metropolis of southern Italy
_____	4. On the straits between the Black and Aegean seas
_____	5. Farthest to the west in continental Europe
_____	6. The capital of the Ukraine
_____	7. The home to about one in every six Swedes
_____	8. The capital of Turkey
_____	9. On straits between the Baltic and the North seas
_____	10. The largest city in the Aegean region

EXTENSIONS

Choose one of the cities on the map and make an outline for a paper on its history. List bibliographical citations for three books that would be useful sources in doing research for this paper.

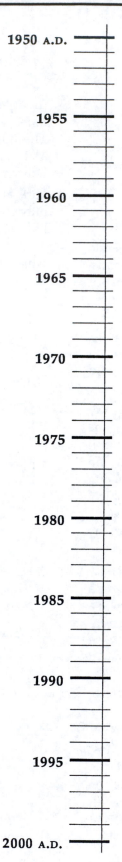

1950 A.D.

1955

1960

1965

1970

1975

1980

1985

1990

1995

2000 A.D.

TOPIC 34
Contemporary Europe: A Chronological Perspective

BACKGROUND

It is time to put your life and the history of your immediate family into the context of contemporary European history. Most students in the United States have family roots that lead directly or indirectly back to Europe. Everyone has a personal past that has been shaped in many ways by events in modern Europe. Comparing the history of the contemporary period in Western civilization with one's own family history thus does more than provide a sense of time. It suggests connections as well, placing each one of us in the river of time where we personally can feel many of its currents.

WORKING WITH SPACE

1. Use the left-hand side of the timeline to note at least ten major events in your own life and the history of your immediate family. Use a marking pen to highlight major turning points in this narrative. Label the column "My Family History."

2. On the other side of the page list an equal number of major events in contemporary Europe. Use your textbook as a source, but note that you will need to rely on news magazines and newspapers for the very latest events. Use a marking pen to highlight major turning points in this story as well.

EXTENSIONS

Write a brief essay on the connections between your life or the story of your family and developments in Europe since 1950. Remember to consider political, cultural, economic, and social factors.

HarperCollins Publishers © 1991

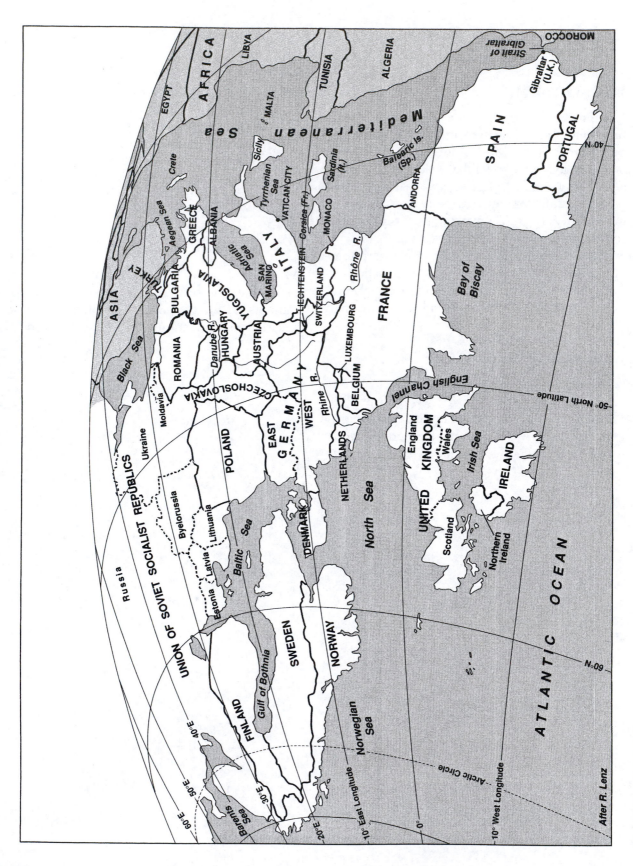

HarperCollins Publishers © 1991

TOPIC 35
Europe Viewed from the Atlantic

BACKGROUND

This map of Europe from a North Atlantic perspective calls forth strings of attachment. North American students looking at European lands from this viewpoint might see a series of ribbons strung across Atlantic connecting the old world to the new. It is a comforting view because it subtly places the Americas in a position of parity, cartographically whispering the old adage about the westward course of progress and civilization.

Thus, although the Atlantic view might have a high degree of relevance to many Americans in the 20th century, it hardly tells the full story. At best it is only one of many maps needed to trace the course of Western civilization. If you can see both the advantages and the limitations of this map, you will be well served, equipped to view with critical eyes every map that you encounter.

WORKING WITH SPACE

1. Note that parts of North Africa and West Asia also appear on this map. Western civilization has its focus in Europe, but draws from sources on the other two continents. In time it also extended its reach, in some fashion, to every part of the globe. The story of Western civilization is always intermixed with the history of the human community.

2. Note how the continent of Europe is cut up by many seas, bays, and inlets. Few places on the continent are more than several hundred miles from the sea. This is often cited as a key factor in the development of a seafaring tradition, a venturesome psychology, and an orientation to the world beyond. Few maps express this point as dramatically as this one.

3. The center of this map is at the 50th parallel. Thus the Arctic Circle is well within the map's perimeter, but the Tropic of Cancer just touches the map at the southeast corner.

4. The importance of the Black and Baltic seas as ways of reaching the interior of Europe is clearly evident.

5. The straits connecting the Black and Aegean seas have been called a great pivot in the development of Western civilization.

PLACES

Which nation is the home for the following artifacts, places, and structures that symbolize aspects of Western civilization?

_____ 1. Stonehenge

_____ 2. Parthenon

_____ 3. Forum

_____ 4. Sancta Sophia

_____ 5. Chartes Cathedral

_____ 6. Gutenberg's printing press

_____ 7. Watt's steam engine

_____ 8. Eiffel Tower

_____ 9. Berlin Wall

_____ 10. First spaceship

EXTENSIONS

Write a brief evaluation of this map as a means to encourage reflective thought on the nature of Western civilization. Try to include both strengths and weaknesses of the map. Conclude with a statement on what this cartographic image means to you.

HarperCollins Publishers © 1991

ANSWERS

TOPIC 1
Places: **3.** France, Spain, Bangladesh, 180th, 90th west;
4. South America, Africa
Working with Space: **1.** fourteen

TOPIC 2
Working with Space: **1.** Mediterranean Sea, Red Sea;
2. Arabian; **3.** Persian, Mediterranean, Egypt; **4.** Black,
Aegean, Mediterranean, Turkey

TOPIC 3
Working with Space: **2.** Suez Canal, Balkan, Aegean, Athens

TOPIC 5
Working with Space: **1.** Norway, Sweden, Findland; **2.** ethnic
or nationality; **3.** Adriatic; **4.** Pyrenees
Places: **1.** Moscow; **2.** London; **3.** Rome; **4.** Lisbon; **5.** Vienna

TOPIC 9
Working with Space: **3.** fountains, windows
Places: **1.** 8; **2.** 7; **3.** 10; **4.** 11; **5.** 12; **6.** 5; **7.** 9; **8.** 1; **9.** 6

TOPIC 10
Places: **1.** Meroe; **2.** Susa; **3.** Celts; **4.** Sinope; **5.** Bactrians

TOPIC 11
Working with Space: **3a.** Caspian Sea; **b.** Persian Gulf;
c. Indian Ocean
Places: **1.** Taprobana; **2.** Fortunate; **3.** Persian Gulf;
4. Western Ocean; **5.** terra incognita

TOPIC 14
Working with Space: **2a.** Oriens; **b.** Occidens; **c.** Miridies;
d. Septentrio; **3.** *Mare Oceanum;* **4.** Asia, Africa, Europe

TOPIC 17
Working with Space: **1.** Paradise; **2.** Pillars of Hercules;
3. Jerusalem; **4.** Euphrates; **5.** Oxus
Places: **1.** yes; **2.** yes; **3.** no; **4.** no; **5.** yes

TOPIC 19
Working with Space: **1.** Tordesillas, Spain, Puerto Rico,
Portugal; **2.** Canibali; **3.** 7448, Zipangri, Japan; **4.** Cuba,
Hispaniola; **5.** Magellan

TOPIC 21
Places: **1.** India Nova or New India; **2.** Hispania Nova or
New Spain; **3.** Mare Rubrum—Red Sea; **4.** Oceanus
Sythicus—Scythean Ocean; **5.** El Stretom de Anian—Strait of
Anian; **6.** Continentis Australis—Austral or Southern
Continent.

TOPIC 22
Places: **1.** Notre Dame cathedral; **2.** Seine; **3.** Louvre;
4. Sorbonne; **5.** Bastille; **6.** Hotel de Ville; **7.** Ste. Genevieve;

8. Pantheon; **9.** Luxembourg; **10.** Place de Louis XV; **11.** des
Invalides; **12.** Champs de Mars

TOPIC 25
Places: **1a.** true, **b.** false, **c.** false, **d.** false, **e.** true;
3a. Liverpool, **b.** Zurich, **c.** Paris, **d.** Berlin or Essen,
e. Ruhr; **4a.** Milan, **b.** Essen; **5a.** iron, hardware, **b.** cotton,
c. linen, **d.** tin and copper, **e.** silk

TOPIC 26
Places: **1.** Denmark, North, Germany, Russian, Norway,
Sweden; **2.** Ottoman, Dalmatia; **3.** Ottoman, Italy, France,
Spain, Gibralter, Malta; **4.** Franco-Prussian; **5.** London

TOPIC 27
Places: **2.** Nile, Zambezi; **3.** Cancer, Capricorn, **4.** Congo,
Victoria

TOPIC 28
Places: **3a.** Stalingrad, **b.** Kasserine Pass, **c.** Liberation of
Rome, **d.** Normandy Invasion, **e.** Battle of the Bulge,
f. Surrender of Berlin; **4.** Morocco; **5.** Normandy, June 6,
June 4, two

TOPIC 30
Places: **1.** Land Power; **2.** Sea Power; **3.** Developed Southern
Ring; **4.** Sea Power; **5.** Maritime Ring; **6.** Sea Power; **7.** Ring
of Underdevelopment; **8.** Sea Power; **9.** Ring of Underdevel-
opment; **10.** Maritime Ring
Working with Space: **1.** Iron Curtain; **2.** North Atlantic Treaty;
3. Japan; **4.** Rimland **5.** Underdevelopment, Poverty,
Martime Ring; **6.** South America, Africa, Australia

TOPIC 31
Places: **8.** China, India, the U.S.S.R., the United States,
Indonesia, Brazil, Japan

TOPIC 32
Working with Space: **1.** Estonian, Latvians, Lithuanians;
2. Belorussian; **3.** 102; **4.** Ukrainian; **5.** southwest; **6.** Black,
Caspian, five; Uzbek; **8.** three; **9.** Turkmen, Tajik, Kirghiz;
10. one, two

TOPIC 33
Places: **1.** Barcelona; **2.** Odessa; **3.** Naples; **4.** Istanbul;
5. Lisbon; **6.** Kiev; **7.** Stockholm; **8.** Ankara; **9.** Copenhagen;
10. Athens

TOPIC 35
Places: **1.** United Kingdom; **2.** Greece; **3.** Rome; **4.** Turkey;
5. France; **6.** Germany; **7.** United Kingdom; **8.** France;
9. Germany; **10.** Soviet Union

90° W

90° E

180°

0°

90° W

Equator

ARCTIC OCEAN

ATLANTIC OCEAN

PACIFIC OCEAN

INDIAN OCEAN

Greenland

CANADA

UNITED STATES

MEXICO

Alaska

Hawaii

NEW ZEALAND

Antarctica

Siberia

UNION OF SOVIET SOCIALIST REPUBLICS (SOVIET UNION)

JAPAN

SOUTH KOREA

CHINA

VIETNAM

PHILIPPINES

THAILAND

INDONESIA

AUSTRALIA

IRAN

PAKISTAN

INDIA

BANGLADESH

SAUDI ARABIA

ETHIOPIA

TURKEY

ISRAEL

EGYPT

ZAIRE

SOUTH AFRICA

WEST GERMANY

GREAT BRITAIN

IRELAND

FRANCE

SPAIN

ITALY

NIGERIA

LIBERIA

BRAZIL

ARGENTINA

PERU

CUBA

CANADA

UNITED STATES

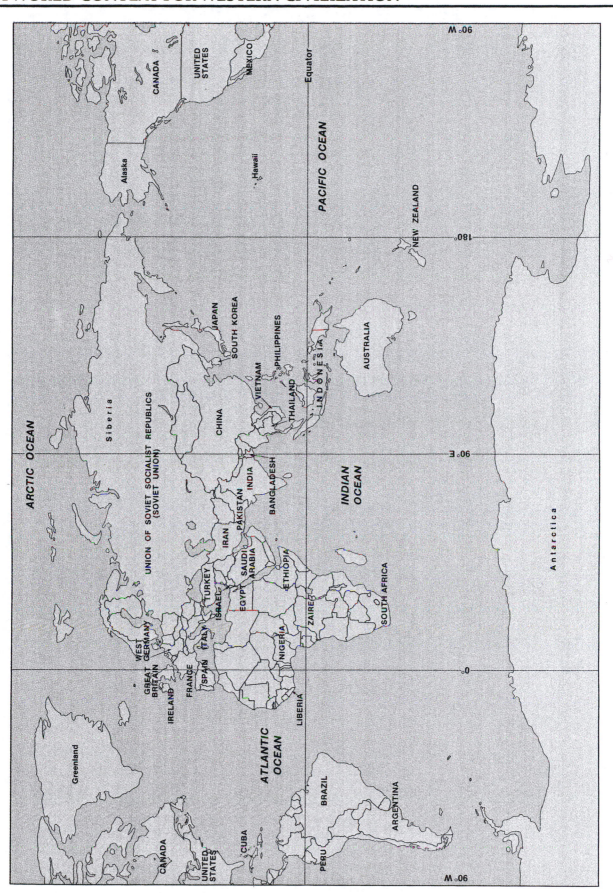

A WORLD CONTEXT FOR WESTERN CIVILIZATION

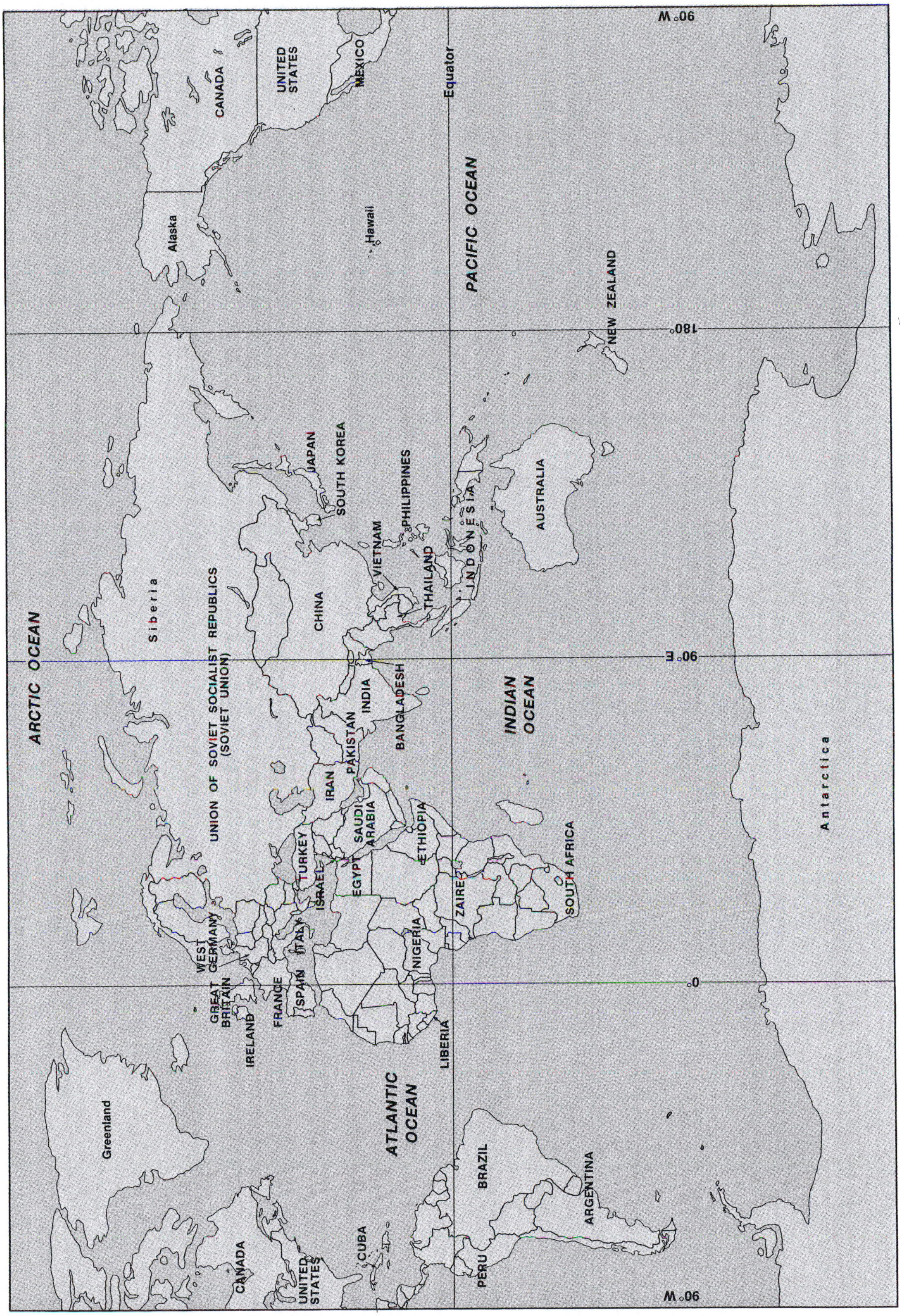

MAPPING WESTERN CIVILIZATION CORRELATIONS

CORRELATIONS WITH KISHLANSKY (1991)

Chapter	Source Maps	Useful Reference Maps	Map Lessons
Introduction	22, 82, 84, 87	1–10	1–6
1	1–9	4	2, 7–9, 12
2	1, 10	4, 5	2, 10, 12
3	10–12, 15	4, 5	2, 10–12
4	13–14	5	3, 12
5	14–17	4, 5, 6	3, 11–12
6	18–20, 22	4	2, 3, 13
7	22–24	4	3, 13–14
8	21	6–8	4, 14, 18
9	19–21, 25–30	3, 5–8	16–18
10	35	3, 5–8	16–18
11	34–36	5–7	6, 11, 18, 24
12	15, 37–39	1–3	1, 5, 6, 11, 19, 24
13	40–42	1, 6–7	4, 20, 24
14	43, 45	6–8	21, 24
15	44	6–8	4, 24
16	46–48	6, 9	4, 22, 24
17	49–51	1–2, 6	1, 5, 21, 24
18	52–54	1–2, 4	1, 4–5, 23–24
19	50, 53, 55–57	2, 6, 8, 10	22–24
20	28–60	4–10	6, 25, 30
21	61–63	1–2, 4–10	4, 26, 30
22	64–66	9–10	4, 26, 30
23	67–69	9–10	4, 27, 30
24	70–72	1–2, 4	30
25	73–75, 82	1–2, 5, 9–10	1, 5, 28, 31
26	76–77, 82	2–4, 9	1, 4, 30, 31
27	79, 82–83	1–2, 10	1, 29–30
28	80–84	1–2, 9–10	1, 29–30
29	82–88	2, 6–10	31–34
30	82–90	1–2, 9–10	31–34
Conclusion	22, 84, 87–88, 90	1–10	31, 35

CORRELATIONS WITH GREAVES, ZALLER, AND ROBERTS (1992)

Chapter	Source Maps	Useful Reference Maps	Map Lessons
Prologue	1–3, 22, 82, 84, 87	1–10	1, 6–7
1	4–9	3–4	2, 8–9
2	10–12	5	3, 10
3	10–12, 15	3–5	10–12
4	13–14	5	3, 12
5	16–20	4–5	4, 12
6	18–24	3–7	15, 18
7	24–27	3–8	4, 18
8	19–30	6–8	13–18
9	28–33	6–8	4, 18
10	34–36	5–8	11, 21
11	40–42	6–8	20, 23
12	37–39	1–2	19, 21
13	43–45	6–8	23
14	43–45	6–8	22–23
15	46–48	6–9	23
16	49–51	1, 10	23
17	52–54	1–2	19, 23
18	55–57	1, 10	22–23
19	58–60	6–10	22–24
20	61–63	10	25
21	64–66	9–10	29
22	67–69	9	5, 26
23	70–73	10	29
24	73–75	1–2	1, 27, 29
25	67–69, 87	1	29
26	76–78	1–2	1, 5, 29
27	82, 87	9–10	29
28	79–81	1, 9	28
29	82–85	1–4, 9	30–32
30	82–90	1–2, 9–10	33–35
Epilogue	87–90	1–2	6, 31, 33–35